617.4706422

D1387049

# Self Assessment in Paediatric
# Musculoskeletal Trauma X-rays

## Also of interest from M&K Publishing

*Books can be ordered online at: www.mkupdate.co.uk*

**Self-assessment in Limb X-ray Interpretation**
ISBN: 978-1-905539-13-0

**Practical Prescribing for Musculoskeletal Practitioners**
ISBN: 978-1-905539-09-3

**Routine Blood Results Explained**
ISBN: 978-1-905539-38-3
Includes new chapter on immunology as applied to the inflammatory autoimmune connective tissue diseases such as rheumatoid arthritis.

**Eye Emergencies: The Practitioner's Guide**
ISBN: 978-1-905539-08-6

**Improving Patient Outcomes**
ISBN: 978-1-905539-06-2

**Management of Pain in Older People Workbook**
ISBN: 978-1-905539-22-2

*Visit the M&K website for a full listing of titles in print and forthcoming books.*

## Forthcoming titles include:

**Paediatric Minor Emergencies**
ISBN: 978-1-905539-35-2

**Primary Care Case Studies for Nurse Practitioners**
ISBN: 978-1-905539-23-9

**Legal Principles and Clinical Practice**
ISBN: 978-1-905539-32-1

**Microbiology and Infection Investigations & Results**
ISBN: 978-1-905539-36-9

Self Assessment in

# Paediatric Musculoskeletal Trauma X-rays

## Karen Sakthivel-Wainford

H.D.C.R (R), PGCert, MSc
Advanced Radiographer Practitioner, Leeds General Infirmary, UK

**Self Assessment in Paediatric Musculoskeletal Trauma X-rays**
Karen Sakthivel-Wainford

ISBN: 978-1-905539-34-5

First published 2008

**British Library Catalogue in Publication Data**
A catalogue record for this book is available from the British Library

**Notice**
Clinical practice and medical knowledge constantly evolve. Standard safety precautions must be followed, but, as knowledge is broadened by research, changes in practice, treatment and drug therapy may become necessary or appropriate. Readers must check the most current product information provided by the manufacturer of each drug to be administered and verify the dosages and correct administration, as well as contraindications. It is the responsibility of the practitioner, utilising the experience and knowledge of the patient, to determine dosages and the best treatment for each individual patient. Any brands mentioned in this book are as examples only and are not endorsed by the Publisher. Neither the Publisher nor the author assume any liability for any injury and/or damage to persons or property arising from this publication.

The Publisher
To contact M&K Publishing write to:
M&K Update Ltd · The Old Bakery · St. John's Street
Keswick · Cumbria CA12 5AS
Tel: 01768 773030 · Fax: 01768 781099
publishing@mkupdate.co.uk
www.mkupdate.co.uk

Designed & typeset by Mary Blood
Printed in England by Footprint Media, Leeds

# Contents

## Acknowledgements

Firstly to Dr Arthur, consultant paediatric radiologist, for the sharing of her knowledge and enthusiasm, which imparted to me an interest in paediatric trauma. Also for her continuing support, particularly with the in-house paediatric trauma courses.

To the radiology departments of Leeds General Infirmary and Wharfedale General Hospital, for their continued support and use of their radiographs in this book.

Lastly, this book is in memory of my father, George Thomas Wainford, and the influence he had on my childhood.

# Introduction

Many nurse practitioners and radiographer practitioners view paediatric trauma radiographs with a certain amount of trepidation. Rightly so – paediatric radiographs can be difficult to interpret, requiring additional learning (additional courses), and experience, but that is the challenge and interest of paediatric trauma.

Children, infants and adolescents are not like 'little adults' with regard to trauma. Firstly, their bone structure and composition is different from adults. The skeleton of the young is more porous, less brittle, the haversian canals are relatively large and their bones contain more water. This results in greater elasticity and plasticity of their bones, leading to various forms of incomplete fracture.

The periosteum in children also differs from that of adults. In a child the periosteum is thicker, more elastic and less firmly bound to bone. The fibres of Sharpey are less numerous and shorter in a child, resulting in them being less effective binders of the periosteum, leading to raised periosteum (in infection). The thicker and more elastic periosteum is more likely to remain at least partially intact and attached to fracture fragments. Thus the periosteum in a child acts as a hinge between fracture fragments, assisting in the reduction and stabilisation of the fracture. Hence non-union in the child is quite rare.

Infants' bones consist of three types: elongated tubular bones, round bones (such as the carpal or tarsal bones) and sesamoid bones (in tendon and articular capsule). Elongated tubular bones are made up of three segments, paired metaphysis, paired epiphysis and diaphysis (shaft of the long bone).

One of the most obvious differences between the skeleton of an adult and child is the degree of maturity. This can be seen by the presence of an epiphyseal ossification centre that is separated from the metaphysis of a long bone by a band of unossified cartilage (the physeal plate). Presence of these growth centres not only modifies the skeletal response to trauma but heightens concern because of the potential for growth disturbance.

This book is written specifically for radiographers, nurse practitioners and radiographer practitioners. It is meant to represent sitting in on a reporting session with a radiologist or reporting radiographer, where you are asked to write a report or comment, but also asked several questions. The book is intended to support whatever course you are attending, or to encourage you to go on that 'paediatric course'.

It starts with an excellent chapter on non-accidental injury (NAI) by Louise Lindsay, a nurse practitioner with an interest in paediatrics, and Joyce M. Clayton, a social worker specialising in children, demonstrating the pathway a suspected NAI case may take from two different perspectives.

Non-accidental injury was thought to be first described by Caffey in 1946 when he was reviewing children with subdural haematomas. Most of the cases of non-accidental injury are brought to medical attention before eighteen months of age, whereas most trauma in children tends to occur after eighteen months of age (when they are more physically active).

Following this there is a series of cases on paediatric trauma, on which you are asked to write reports, plus sometimes answer a few questions. The cases are divided into eight groups, trauma radiographs of the wrist and hand (15 cases), elbow and forearm (10 cases), shoulder (10 cases), foot and ankle (15 cases), knee (10 cases), hip and pelvis (10 cases), rest of the axial skeleton (9 cases). The last group of cases is a mixture of paediatric trauma cases (21 cases).

I have concentrated on the areas of paediatric trauma that more commonly present to an emergency department; hence there are more cases of foot and ankle, and wrist and hand, than other areas, as these are the most frequent emergency department attendees. Also these are areas radiographer practitioners and nurse practitioners are most likely to be reviewing.

The cases have all been anonymised, hence there are no names and sometimes no anatomical markers. This also sometimes results in some of the radiographic anatomy not being present. Each case has some appropriate clinical history with it, but this is often not the original clinical history in order for the patient to remain anonymous.

Lastly there is a list of texts and journals I have found particularly useful in researching paediatric trauma. As for whether all the cases have trauma demonstrated on the radiograph or not, that is for you to decide.

# 1.

# Non-accidental injury

## The Nurse Practitioner's perspective

Louise Lindsay

RN, ENP Sister

This chapter covers the role of the Emergency Nurse Practitioner (ENP) in the care of children with non-accidental injuries (NAIs) and will cover some of the laws and legislation surrounding this issue, clinical signs to look out for and what the ENP needs to do if he or she suspects NAI. There are many issues within child protection and I propose to deal with the key points the ENP should be aware of.

Every week in England and Wales at least one child dies following cruelty (National Society for the Prevention of Cruelty to Children, 2004). The people most likely to die a violent death are babies under one year who are four times more likely to be killed than the average person (Youd, 2005). However, abuse can occur at any age in a child's life, in any culture and within any social background and environment. Therefore ENPs need to be vigilant to the possibility of NAI for all children attending a minor injuries unit (MIU). All ENPs must be familiar with and follow legislation and their organisation's procedures, policies and protocols for safeguarding and promoting the welfare of children in their area and know who to contact in their organisation to express concerns about a child's welfare. This can be very complex and therefore daunting for any healthcare professional as they have to gain a clear understanding of what the implications and impacts are so that they can include these in their working practices. Ultimately, the ENP is accountable and responsible legally and professionally to themselves, to the patients, for the safeguarding and welfare of the child and its family, and to the employing institution and the nursing profession. The Government issued a non-statutory guidance booklet in 2006 on 'What to do if you're worried a child is being abused' (Department of Health, 2006a). This is very helpful for understanding and working within the requirements of the Children Act 1989 and 2004.

So, what does safeguarding and promoting the welfare of children mean? The Children Act, (p. 8, 3.1) gives the following definition:

● protecting children from maltreatment

- preventing impairment of children's health or development
- ensuring that children are growing up in circumstances consistent with the provision of safe and effective care, and
- undertaking that role so as to enable those children to have optimum life chances and to enter adulthood successfully.

The Children's Act 1989/2004 offers the most comprehensive legislative framework with regard to the rights, care and protection of children and the responsibilities of those who care for them. There are other laws and legislation and each geographical NHS area is responsible for developing their own procedures following that legal framework. The procedures for the area in which I work are detailed by the Leeds Local Safeguarding Children Board (LSCB) in the Inter-Agency Child Protection Procedures. It is now a mandatory requirement that all ENPs achieve the Level 1 Child Protection E-Learning Module (2006) produced by the Child Protection Health Advisory Group, Trustwide Child Protection Steering Group and the Leeds Named Nurses: Child Protection Group which covers all relevant areas of child protection. All ENPs should be aware of the West Yorkshire Safeguarding Procedures which can be accessed from www.leedslscb.org.uk.

Also the Children Safeguarding Nursing Team within Leeds Teaching Hospitals NHS Trust (LTHT) produced a supporting Paediatric Liaison Resource File. This is easy to follow and contains the *Framework for the Assessment of Children and their Families* (DOH, 2000) which is an essential tool for the ENP to use when working towards safeguarding and promoting child welfare (see Figure 1.1). Any one of the three domains in the triangle within the Framework may raise an issue about a child. The Resource File also lists all the healthcare professionals, their areas of responsibility, names and telephone numbers, together with flowcharts of actions to take when concerned about a presenting child or their family. It is also the ENP's responsibility to keep up to date with all changes as they arise by research, reading and attending relevant courses and by liaising appropriately with other healthcare professionals. ENPs should work within the Assessment Framework. If an ENP suspects non-accidental injury, he or she must follow all protocols, policies, procedures and guidelines on child protection set out by their organisation.

Armed with all the above, the ENP needs to be able to identify an NAI. There are many definitions of child abuse. Abuse and neglect are forms of maltreatment of a child. Somebody may abuse or neglect a child by inflicting harm, or by failing to act to prevent harm. Children may be abused in a family or in an institutional or community setting by those known to them or, more rarely, by a stranger. They may be abused by an adult or adults, or another child or children (HM Government, 2006b, p. 37, 1.29).

As soon as a child and family attend the MIU it is the responsibility of all the multi-disciplinary team to pass on all observations and information to the ENP. Any information could be vital for the ENP's assessment and safeguarding of the child. The

**4**

ENP may be the first professional a child and family come into contact with.

Youd (2005) asserted that all emergency nurses, not only those working in traditional emergency departments but also and particularly those with new autonomous roles in walk-in centres, MIUs, children centres and primary care environments, may be the only professionals seeing particular children during care episodes (p. 15). She also states 'front line emergency nurses must ensure they have the necessary core skills, knowledge and competencies in assessing and treating children' (p. 16).

Figure 1.1 **Factors affecting child welfare**

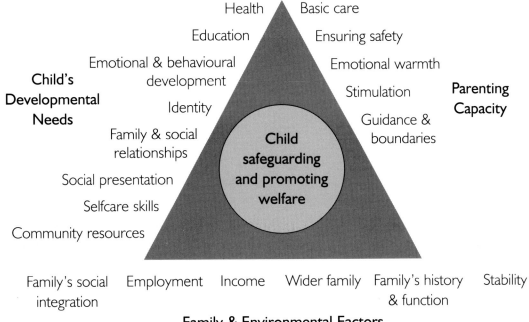

The ENP should start the clinical assessment by interacting professionally, positively and in a friendly manner using good communication skills in an effort to put the child and family at ease. The ENP should communicate with the child in a way that is appropriate to their age, understanding and preference. Whaley and Wong (1991) indicate that knowledge of development theory will enable the nurse to choose words that are appropriate for the child's chronological age and anticipated understanding. The skill involved is not only using the correct words but also interpreting verbal and non-verbal feedback from the child. Morgan (1991) states that using the correct approach to an injured child will help in gaining the child's co-operation and trust. The ENP also needs to gain the trust of the family. Dolan (1997) reminds us that no child can be thought of in isolation from their family. The assessment includes obtaining the history of the presenting complaint, i.e. which part of

**5**

the body, what has happened, when, how and where it was witnessed. Throughout the assessment the ENP should monitor the following:

- interactions and reactions of the child with the family, looking for any odd behaviour
- compatibility of the history with the developmental stage of the child
- how the child looks and whether there are signs of failure to thrive
- whether the mechanism of the injury fits with the history and injury
- whether there has been a delay in attending the MIU for treatment
- whether there is a history of previous attendances at the MIU or main site A & E departments
- what the child says about the accident
- whether the account is vague or lacking in detail
- whether the parent's and child's accounts of the injury are the same
- whether staff members within the MIU have been given different accounts of what happened; this is why it is vital the multidisciplinary team shares information.

This approach is supported by Wynne (1994) who states that the presentation of history may give clues or raise the question of abuse.

None of the above is foolproof and there can be many other factors that may come to the ENP's attention during the assessment. If there are previous attendances, the ENP needs to know what these were for and documentation about previous attendances should be reviewed. Also, the ENP must take into account multiple previous attendances to MIUs and emergency departments as these could show a pattern of abuse.

The ENP then carries out a thorough clinical examination of the child, in accordance with local guidelines, whilst being aware of the common sites for NAIs. It is of great value during the examination if the ENP, with the help of other colleagues and involving the family, can use distraction techniques with the child. According to Gay (1992) distraction, relaxation, imagery and reinforcement are all effective ways of reducing stress in children undergoing procedures. In all cases the ENP should identify any bruises of varying ages and colours, swellings, wounds, deformities, bony tenderness or any abnormalities. It is important for the ENP always to observe the child's reactions to the clinical examination and to look for any signs of neglect, other injuries or other concerns. If the ENP observes a failure to thrive or has other concerns then they should weigh the child and chart this using the centile chart creating a base record for future reference. Greenidge (1997) believes the knowledge of the related anatomy and physiology is vital to ensure an accurate, systematic and holistic assessment. The ENP should gain an impression of the type of injury and decide on the next plan for the child. This could be requesting an x-ray before decision making, referring to the main hospital site or other healthcare professionals for further assessment, or on-site diagnosis, treating and discharging. If the ENP decides an x-ray is required, this has to be carried out in accordance with their organisation's policy for referral of patients to radiology, also taking into account their local guidelines and protocols, and must not go out of these boundaries. The ENP should stay within their Code of Conduct and Scope of Professional Practice (UKCC, 1992a, 1992b). If the area for x-ray is not within the ENP's protocol this must be referred to a main hospital site for an A & E doctor to review. If a child has been x-rayed on site, the ENP must make a clinical decision based upon the radiograph and clinical findings and then follow this up with the appropriate action. For the ENP to interpret and report on x-rays they must have the appropriate training and authorisation and, if not, the x-ray must be reported on by a radiographer or authorised colleague. Should an NAI be suspected, then the ENP should begin to document concerns and follow documented procedures. In the first instance, this could be liaising with school nurses, health visitors, GPs and other healthcare professionals by telephone, to ascertain if the family have a social worker, any previous history of problems or if the child is subject to a child protection plan. A list of children who are subject to a child protection plan is accessible from Children and Family Social Care. This is managed by Safeguarding Children Senior Co-ordinators (LSCB, 2007). These general enquiries can give the ENP valuable information before any approach is made to the family or any further action is taken.

Wynne (1994) states that staff working in this difficult field must be trained and supported. The work is skilled, time consuming and emotionally taxing. The consequences for the child and family if the abuse is not recognised or is wrongly diagnosed are considerable.

ENPs should bear in mind that a referral for a child could result in access to services under Section 17 of the Children Act 1989 for family support before the situation deteriorates to a level where the child must be referred for protection under Section 47 of the Act. If unsure, the ENP should always liaise with the Children Safeguarding Nursing Team. If the x-ray interpretation of a suspicious fracture indicates that this could be an NAI, this must be reported to the Children Safeguarding Nursing Team and Children and Young People's Social Care.

After gathering all the information, if a cause for concern with Child Protection issues exists, this falls under Section 47 of the Children Act 1989/2004 (Child Protection). The objective of local authority enquiries conducted under Section 47 is to determine whether action is needed to promote and safeguard the welfare of the child or children who are the subject of enquiries. In the great majority of cases children remain with families and, even if concerns about abuse or neglect are substantiated, enquiries should be conducted in a way that allows for constructive relationships with families (LSCB, 2007).

At this point, the ENP must relate their professional concerns to parents and carers and be prepared to answer questions openly and honestly, unless to do so would affect the safety and welfare of the child. If an ENP wishes to refer to Children and Young People's Social Care because it is felt a child is at risk then it is good practice to always seek the consent of the parent to make that referral, unless to do so would put the child at risk. If the ENP feels a child is at risk of significant harm they do not require the consent of the parent to refer. Likewise, if the child is already subject to a child protection plan there is no need to gain consent. In *Working Together to Safeguard Children* (Department of Health, 1999, p, 40, para 5.6), it states 'while professionals should seek, in general to discuss any concerns with the family and, where possible, seek their agreement to making a referral to social services, this should only be done where such discussion and agreement-seeking will not place a child at increased risk'. The powers, duties and roles of agencies involved, and their own legal rights, should be explained to the parents. Care should always be taken if the ENP is aware of a situation with the child and/or family which could become volatile and he or she should not put themselves in a vulnerable position.

If the ENP is aware that a social carer is already involved with the family then they should be informed of the cause for concern during office hours or to the Emergency Duty Team (EDT) outside office hours. If there is no previous social care involvement the ENP should contact the duty social care team on the call centre number during office hours. This should be documented and the ENP should keep a copy for their own records and fax a copy to the appropriate professional and agencies who require the information. The ENP should also indicate whether they have informed the child and/or parents of the referral and whether the child and/or parents have indicated their agreement to information about them being shared between agencies for the purposes of assessment.

The individual ENP continues to be responsible for raising their concerns and communicating with health visitors, school nurses, the Children Safeguarding Nursing Team and Young People's Social Care, EDT social carers and the police. They should make all the referrals themselves and not assume that these will be done by someone else; otherwise there is a risk of breakdown in communication and a child could become at risk. It is best practice to carry out all these referrals within 24–48 hours.

The child must be referred by the ENP to medical staff within their organisation at the main hospital's emergency department. It is good practice and necessary for the ENP to liaise verbally with a senior A&E doctor, senior paediatric registrar and any other specialist doctor as appropriate, together with the paediatric area. Also the ENP should ensure the Children Safeguarding Nursing Team are made aware. Again this communication is essential for safeguarding the welfare of the child.

It is crucial that all assessments, examinations, clinical findings, descriptions and drawings of injuries are documented and the appropriate proformas are used in all cases. Comprehensive, accurate and timely documentation is necessary for high-quality healthcare (Cooper, 2000).

The Trustwide *Child Protection Policy* (Child Protection Health Advisory Group,43 2006) states that accurate record keeping is an essential element which must underpin child protection work. ENPs must remember that the function of accurate record keeping is not only to enhance seamless care but is also evidentially crucial. The Policy also states that effective child protection work relies not only on excellent interagency communication but also on the quality of recorded information. It not only clarifies the nature, extent and the development of concerns but also helps to identify patterns of behaviour. In addition, it states that basic principles of record keeping must be adhered to and must be contemporaneous in nature, e.g. entries must be legible, written in black ink, signed with name printed beneath signature, dated and timed. Also any record of the child's words should be verbatim and not an interpretation of what the child meant. If the ENP asks the child questions, these should be included in the record also.

Once everything has been completed, the ENP arranges for the safe and secure transportation of the child or family to the main hospital emergency department. This is a crucial point to prevent further risk or harm to the child. If the child is suspected to have suffered abuse this may involve organising an ambulance. If abuse is confirmed the police may already be involved and safe transport or transfer is mandatory in these cases.

The ENP may be the first professional the child and family come into contact with and therefore plays a crucial role in identifying suspected safeguarding issues or abuse or NAIs in the first instance. This can be very challenging, complex and time consuming but also very valuable and rewarding. The ENP has a frontline role in protecting the child and preventing further risk or harm. Within my own area of work all staff are constantly vigilant, sharing information and highlighting to each other any concerns or anomalies which may arise with the presenting child or family. This multidisciplinary team effort is of great value and importance and should be occurring in all work environments that provide services for children. Is this happening in your workplace? In addition, the legislation, procedures, policies and protocols are available to support ENPs and multidisciplinary teams in their work and they should consult their own safeguarding policy and procedures for further guidance. Added to this, with the efficient child protection networks that exist there is no excuse not to be effective in the child protection process. This effectiveness could prevent the further harm or future death of a child.

*Working Together to Safeguard Children* states that 'safeguarding and promoting welfare of children – and in particular protecting them from significant harm – depends on effective joint working between agencies and professionals that have different roles and expertise' (Department of Health, 2006b, p. 33, 1.14). Junior and senior staff have different roles in safeguarding individual children. 'Individual children, especially some of the most vulnerable children and those at greater risk of social exclusion, will need co-ordinated help from healthcare professionals' (1.14). 'In order to achieve this joint

**9**

working, there need to be constructive relationships between individual workers, promoted and supported by all' (1.15). We should all work together to safeguard and protect the child's welfare and there should always be partnership with families and colleagues throughout the care process.

# The Social Worker's perspective

Joyce M. Clayton

Regional Paediatric Specialist Social Worker

Paediatric x-ray interpretation is a crucial part of dealing with a non-accidental injury. This x-ray is evidence and gives feedback to the paediatric consultant who can then review their medical and social information and decide within a strategy discussion with Social Care and other relevant agencies whether this is indeed a non-accidental injury.

The role of social workers in non-accidental injuries is a particularly difficult one. It has been made more difficult by attitudes of some parts of the media. It seems that in some people's opinion social workers cannot do right; they either fail to protect children from injury, or when they act to prevent a child being injured they are accused of wrecking families lives and have been described as 'do-gooders' and 'interfering busybodies'.

## The national agenda

Since 2003 the Government has been outlining its *Every Child Matters* agenda. This develops a new approach for delivering services to children, young people and families. It will radically change the way we work together, from teachers and social workers to voluntary organisations and primary care trusts.

The Government published its *Every Child Matters* green paper in 2003 as a response to Lord Laming's inquiry into the death of Victoria Climbié. He identified poor integration and communication between services and a lack of accountability as serious failings that contributed to the death of Victoria.

A wide range of national legislation and guidance now informs *Every Child Matters,* including:

- The Children Act 2004
- The National Service Framework for Children, Young People and Maternity Services
- The Five-Year Education Strategy
- The Childcare Strategy
- Choosing Health
- Youth Matters.

**10**

The Leeds Safeguarding Board consists of the following membership:

- Leeds City Council Social Care Department
- Leeds City-wide Health Services
- Leeds Mental Health Services NHS Trust
- Education Leeds
- Leeds City Council Department of Legal Services
- Leeds City Council Neighbourhood and Housing Services
- Leeds City Council Department of Leisure Services
- Leeds City Council Early Years Service
- West Yorkshire Police
- West Yorkshire Probation Service
- NSPCC (National Society for the Prevention of Cruelty to Children)
- Voluntary agencies
- Leeds Inter-Agency Project Women and Violence
- CAFCASS (Children and Family Court Advisory Support Service)
- Youth Offending
- Connexions West Yorkshire
- HM Wetherby young offenders unit.

The above agencies play an essential part in the process of protection of children. The work of the statutory and voluntary agencies is co-ordinated by the Leeds Safeguarding Board. The agencies meet regularly to review existing policies and services, and monitor child protection activity in the city.

## Levels of intervention model for safeguarding children and young people

In order to offer a framework for child protection work, the following model provides a tool for identifying clearly the purpose of any interventions.

- **Preventative:** Work that aims to minimise the risks of children being abused or abusing other people both now and in the future, including work with families under pressure or stress.
- **Protective:** Work that aims to protect children from abuse when concerns have been identified, including enabling children to protect themselves where possible and seek support if and when they need to. It includes developing understanding, skills, information and child protection procedures that aim to protect children from abuse, and providing access to family support.
- **Supportive:** Work that aims to support children who have experienced any form of abuse, aiming to meet their needs, support the process of recovery, minimise the possibility of abuse occurring again or it contributing to learnt behaviours.

## A case study

I will explain the process of child protection and investigating a non-accidental injury using an anonymous family. The presenting family are mother Anna aged 25 years, father Robert aged 29 years and baby Tony aged 5 months, the couple's first child. Tony's parents are married and therefore both have parental responsibility for him according to the law.

Anna has brought baby Tony to the emergency department screaming. She herself is distressed and crying. Staff have great difficulty ascertaining what has happened because of the distress of both mother and child. This is complicated because Anna cannot speak or understand English. Robert follows and is angry that Anna has brought baby Tony to the hospital. He is so angry staff have called security to calm the situation so that Tony can be medically examined. Robert is requested to calm himself or the police will be called. He is told that his threatening behaviour to his wife and intimidating attitude to the staff will not be tolerated. He is oblivious to the fact that his pattern of behaviour is emotionally damaging to babies, children and young people, primarily to his own son and others waiting in the accident and emergency department. On presentation to hospital there often is anger and frustration but the child's well-being and protection is paramount. There should always be respect for culture, class, disability, illness and religion to safeguard the child's welfare.

At this point it is urgent for an interpreter to be sought to be present during baby Tony's medical or, if that is not possible, a telephone link. During the interpreted discussion and examination the consultant ascertains that Anna has been at work and Robert was babysitting. Robert informs the doctor and nurse that baby Tony rolled off his parents' bed onto the carpeted floor. He was screaming when Robert picked him up and put him in his cot. He was still screaming in his cot when his mother Anna returned from work. Robert was downstairs drinking heavily and watching television. Anna picked up their son and ran to the hospital. On examination the doctor suspects a fractured femur. He requests an x-ray and the outcome is a spiral fracture of baby Tony's femur. This injury is serious and in my experience can be caused by a forceful pulling, twisting action. A skeletal survey would follow to check that there are no other fractures, new or old and healed. Baby Tony is admitted to the children's orthopaediac ward to have his leg put in traction. As his parents are agreeing to his admission he is now in a 'safe place' whilst information is gathered and an enquiry commenced.

The nursing sister contacts the social care office and asks if the family are known. Past computer records inform that baby Tony has already had a bruise on his forehead at age four months. The explanation was accepted as it was feasible. However at that time Anna had gone into a women's hostel for a week after a domestic argument that was attended by the police. She was observed there to be a caring mother who was attached to her baby son. She returned to Robert after he had pleaded to give him another chance. As the explanation for the fracture is not compatible with the father's story of a fall from the bed, there now needs to be further investigation to protect baby Tony.

The next process is a strategy meeting, usually held at the hospital. The duty team manager chairs and records the minutes of the meeting. The agencies involved need to be coordinated from health, education, police, social care, the voluntary sector and youth justice services if appropriate. This process is a shared responsibility needing accurate information that is non-judgemental. It is not just Social Care's responsibility to safeguard children and young people.

If a baby, child or young person is brought to the accident and emergency department of the hospital with an injury and there is no matching explanation for that injury then it is in the child's best interests that a Section 47 enquiry commences. This action places a duty on the following:

● local authority
● local education authority
● housing authority
● health authority, strategic health authority or National Health Service trust
● the person authorised by the Secretary of State; they are to help an authority with its enquiries in cases where there is reasonable cause to suspect that a child is suffering, or is likely to suffer, significant harm.

As professionals we are all working together to safeguard children. They all deserve the opportunity to achieve their full potential. This is set out in the five outcomes within the *Every Child Matters Children and Young People's Plan*, and are as follows:

● to stay safe
● to be healthy
● to enjoy and achieve
● to make a positive contribution
● to achieve economic well-being.

Becoming a parent or carer (with parental responsibility) does not mean that there is a perfect way to bring up children. Good parenting involves caring for children and providing them with basic needs. This means giving children love and warmth, keeping them safe and providing them with stimulation needed for their development. This then assists them to meet their potential within their capabilities. This is equivalent to a stable home environment where parents and carers give consistent appropriate guidance and boundaries.

Babies, young children and adolescents are more challenging than they ever have been. Parents and carers need support and empowerment within that role. As professionals we

**13**

should acknowledge that parents asking for help is a positive step and not a sign of failure, which is how many feel when they need support.

As in the Children Act 1989 and 2004, a child is anyone who has not yet reached their eighteenth birthday. 'Child' therefore means 'young person'. The fact that a young person has reached the age of sixteen years, living independently or in foster care, in the armed forces, prison or a young offenders' institution, does not change his or her status or entitlement to services or protection under the Children Act of 1989.

A child or young person being brought to the accident and emergency department will initially be seen by the triage nurse. The information gathered at this stage has to be accurate and recorded. If the explanation by the parent or carer does not satisfactorily match the injury then the social care department should be contacted. In the city of Leeds, this would be Hospital Team during office hours for the hospitals and, outside of office hours, the Emergency Duty Team. This referral should be a rapid response for the child's safety and a written referral highlighting the concerns should follow and also a medical report.

In good practice, baby Tony's parents should be informed and have a discussion regarding this decision. There is often anger and frustration at this time but the child's well-being and protection is paramount, during and after the enquiry. Being honest with parents and giving them feedback after each stage is crucial in working alongside the family and ultimately the child or young person. Respecting culture, class, disability, illness and religion is all part of safeguarding the child's welfare.

At the strategy meeting, the accident and emergency staff may have only just met the family; however the school, family doctor, and health visitor may have known the family for years and can bring crucial background information to assist the discussion. This information is unknown at presentation at the hospital.

After the strategy meeting the family needs to be seen straight away as anxieties are heightened. Families need to be seen, and treated with respect and honesty and not left in 'limbo'. There is no way of minimising this stressful time; however the best interests of the child are paramount for their health and safety.

Following baby Tony's strategy meeting an initial assessment will be completed within seven working days and a recommendation made. This assessment is completed under the *Framework for the Assessment of Children and their Families* (Department of Health, 2000). If there is still concern then a child protection conference would be held to bring his parents and professionals together to share information, reports, discussion and plan how to safeguard this child following his non-accidental injury. Will the child be safe if he goes home? Sometimes parents or carers will agree that the child can be looked after by relatives whilst a risk assessment is completed over a period of 35 working days. If parents refuse then Social Care has the responsibility to seek legal advice to safeguard the child. This then actions orders from the court to assist the social care agency to continue to work with parents and carers within the legal framework.

In baby Tony's case the strategy meeting of professionals and the social worker's initial assessment highlighted the fact that Anna had not been present when this injury happened to her son, as she was at work. She had not delayed in presenting him at the hospital and agreed to work with professionals with a Core Assessment, over 35 working days. Her husband Robert was arrested and interviewed by the police and within that time he admitted that he had lost his temper with his baby son. He agreed to get help with his drink and temper problem. Anna decided that her son had to come first and that she would separate from her husband until he proved he had changed. A contract was signed by Anna that she would not leave their son on his own with his father and would continue to work within a family support plan with the social care staff. This contract is not legally binding. However if parents or carers do not work in partnership with the plan it can be a tool to take to court to show that they had a written explanation of why there was a need to work together, for the welfare of their child.

The enquiry into the death of Victoria Climbie, and the Chief Inspector's safeguarding reports brought forward the shortcomings of not intervening early enough, poor co-ordination, a failure to share information, and the absence of anyone with a strong sense of accountability. These informed the Green Paper entitled *Every Child Matters* and the Children Act 2004. The Department of Health published practice guidance to assist practitioners to work together to safeguard children from harm, known as 'What to do if you are worried a child is being abused' (DOH, 2006b).

Let's continue to communicate together and share our concerns so that all children are safeguarded.


*Louise Lindsay spent six years working as a senior nurse in A & E and five years as an emergency nurse practitioner within the NHS. She is currently an ENP in a busy minor injury unit and is the unit's Link Nurse for child surveillance.*

*Joyce Clayton has been a social worker at St James University Hospital in Leeds for over 18 years, involved in child protection and child care social work. She has worked with the Child Development Team, Child Protection Team and is currently the Paediatric Hepatology Transplant Unit, Regional Paediatric Specialist Team Social Worker, a credited practice teacher, and works on call for the Emergency Duty Social Care Team.*

## References

Child Protection Health Advisory Group, Trustwide Child Protection Steering Group and the Leeds Named Nurses Child Protection Group (Sept 2002/2006). *Child Protection Policy/Child Protection Report Writing Guidelines*, Level 1 Child Protection E-Learning Module.

Cooper, M.A. (2000). 'Emergency Nurse Practitioners, Development of an Audit Tool' in *Emergency Nurse*, 8, (5): 34–9.

Department of Health (1999). *Working Together to Safeguard Children*, London: DH.

Department of Health (2000). *Framework for the Assessment of Children and their Families*, London: DH.

Department of Health (2006a). 'What to do if you're worried a child is being abused' in *Every Child Matters – Change for Children* (Non-Statutory Guidance), London: DH.

Department of Health (2006b). 'Working together to safeguard children, A guide to inter-agency working to safeguard and promote the welfare of children' in *Every Child Matters – Change for Children* (Statutory Guidance), London: Department of Health.

Dolan, K. (1997). 'Children in accident and emergency' in *Accident and Emergency Nursing*, 5 (2): 88–91.

Gay, J. (1992). 'A painful experience' in *Nursing Times*, 88 (25): 32–5.

Greenidge, P. (1997). 'Requesting and interpreting x-rays in A&E' in *Emergency Nurse*, 5 (5): 31–6.

Leeds Local Safeguarding Children Board (2007). Inter-Agency Child Protection Procedures. Managed by the Leeds Safeguarding Children Senior Co-ordinators on an ongoing basis, Leeds: LSCB.

Leeds Safeguarding Children Board (2007). West Yorkshire Safeguarding Procedures for Children, available at www.leedslscb.org.uk (last accessed 15.3.2008).

Leeds Teaching Hospital NHS Trust (2007). Paediatric Liaison Resource File. Produced by the Children Safeguarding Nursing Team within and managed by them on an ongoing basis, LTHT.

Leeds Teaching Hospital NHS Trust (2003). Policy for Referral of Patients to Radiology from Nurse Practitioners, Accident & Emergency/MIUs, LTHT.

Morgan, M. (1991). 'Nursing management of the injured child' reprinted in Davis, J. 'Children in accident and emergency, parental perceptions of the quality of care, Part 2' in *Accident and Emergency Nursing* (1995) 3 (2): 89–91.

National Society for the Prevention of Cruelty to Children (2004). *Child abuse in Britain*, available at www.nspcc.org.uk/html/home/whatwedo/childabuseinbritain.htm (last accessed 15.3.2008).

United Kingdom Central Council (1992). *The Code of Professional Conduct for Nurses Midwives and Health Visitors*. London: UKCC.

United Kingdom Central Council (1992). *Scope of Professional Practice*. London: UKCC.

Whaley, L. and Wong, D. (1991). 'Nursing care of infants and children' reprinted in Wood, I. 'Communicating with children in A&E – what skills does the nurse need?' in *Accident and Emergency Nursing*, 1997, 5 (3):137–41.

Wynne, J. (1994). 'The construction of child abuse in the accident and emergency department' in Clocke, C. *Health Visitors and Nurses*. Harlow: Longman, 75–87.

Youd, J. (2005). 'Lost generation' in *Emergency Nurse*, 12: 15–17.

# 2.

# Wrist and hand trauma

# Case 1

Patient fell onto outstretched hand (FOOSH), now painful wrist.

Describe the radiographs.

In which of the three areas of long tubular bones is this type of injury normally located?

# Answer to Case 1

There is a torus fracture of the dorsal aspect of the distal radial metaphysis. There is a loss in the normal volar angulation of the distal radius (normally volarly angulated by 10 to 15 degrees). Loss of the normal angulation of the distal radius is often a clue to injury. Torus fractures commonly occur in the metaphysis.

**Torus** is a Latin word meaning round swelling or protuberance. A torus fracture is a buckling of the cortex of the bone produced by compression forces. A series of micro-fractures in the crystalline structure of young bones allows this buckling to occur. When the child falls on their outstretched hand (as in this case) the buckling occurs on the dorsal aspect of the radius. If the child fell with the same amount of force causing the supinated hand to be compressed against the volar aspect of the wrist, then the torus fracture would be on the volar aspect of the wrist (a Smith's type fracture in an adult).

Torus fracture of dorsal aspect of distal radial metaphysis

Remember 'volar' refers to the anterior aspect of the forearm. It is essential when reviewing forearm radiographs that you look extremely carefully at the wrist and elbow as well as the length of the forearm, as many injuries occur at these joints.

In the young, the ends of the bones are often regarded as the weak areas due to the predominance of physeal plates there.

A fall on the outstretched hand results in different injuries depending on the age of the patient:

- under 5 years of age  – supracondylar fracture of the distal humerus
- 5 to 10 years of age – transverse fracture of the metaphysis of the distal radius, 2 to 4 centimetres proximal to the growth plate (maybe an incomplete type fracture)
- 10 to 16 years of age – epiphyseal separation of the distal radius (most  commonly a Salter Harris ll)
- 18 to 35 years of age – fracture of the scaphoid or other carpal bone
- 40 years plus – a Colles type fracture.

These age ranges can be useful in the search for an injury, but remember they are meant only as guidelines, and children can have unusual or unexpected fractures for their age group.

## Case 2

Patient fell from climbing frame, injuring wrist, unsure of mechanism of injury.

Describe the radiographs.

What is the name for this type of injury?

## Answer to Case 2

There is a break in the cortex on the volar aspect of the distal radial metaphysis. This is a greenstick fracture. A classic greenstick fracture is a result of a bending or angulation force that places the convex side of the bone in tension and the concave side in compression.

This results in an incomplete transverse fracture being produced on the convex cortex by the tension forces which extends to the middle of the shaft, involving half the circumference of the bone, then turns at right angles at its most medial extent to create a vertical or longitudinal split. Often the longitudinal or vertical split is not visualised radiographically. This injury is meant to be like the bending of a twig, hence the name greenstick fracture.

# Case 3

Patient fell onto outstretched hand, now painful wrist.

Describe the radiograph.

What is the name for this type of injury?

What is a bow type fracture, and where do they most commonly occur?

# Answer to Case 3

Unfortunately there was no anterior posterior view available. There is an incomplete fracture of the volar aspect of the distal radius (metaphysis area), and a torus fracture of the dorsal aspect of the distal radius. This is called a 'lead pipe' fracture, analogous to the fracture that occurs in a lead pipe when bent. It is a fairly uncommon injury that normally occurs in the metaphysis and is a combination of an incomplete fracture of one cortex and a torus fracture of the other side. Note also there is dorsal angulation of the distal radius instead of the normal volar angulation.

Due to the normal elasticity and plasticity of young bones they may be bent without fracture; these are called bow fractures. If a child's bone is bent with a certain amount of force it will bend and return to normal; this is called elastic deformation. If you increase the force then the bone will bend and stay bent; this is plastic deformation and results in a bow fracture. Some authors represent this phenomenon by a stress/strain curve. If you increase the force further on the bone then you reach failure point and this results in a fracture. To conclude, with a bow fracture the force involved exceeds the amount of elastic strain that allows complete recovery of the normal shape but is less than is required to cause a complete fracture. Bow fractures occur most commonly in the radius and ulna, but may also occur in the fibula. If the curvature is severe in the forearm it may interfere with rotational movements. If the fibula is severely affected it may interfere with proper alignment and apposition of an associated fracture of the tibia. Periosteal new bone formation is produced on the concave side, where histologically a series of microfractures occur.

# Case 4

Patient was playing netball, and hyperextended the thumb.
Now pain in thumb.

Describe the radiographs.

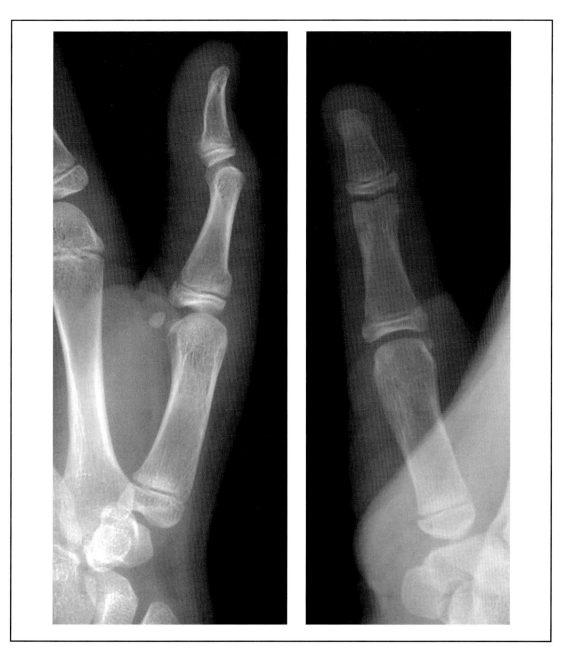

# Answer to Case 4

There appears to be a torus type fracture (a buckling of the metaphysis) on the dorsal aspect of the proximal phalanx metaphysis. However on closer inspection at the site of the torus fracture there is a lucent line that probably transverses into the physeal plate. A fracture that involves the physeal plate and the metaphysis is classified as a Salter Harris II fracture (see Case 5 for Salter Harris classification).

The physeal plate is made of four distinct zones, starting from the metaphysis: zone 1 is resting/mother cells, 2 is proliferating cells, 3 is hypertrophic cells, 4 is area of provisional calcification. Zones 1 and 2 lie in the matrix and have collagen fibres running through, which strengthens these zones. Zone 4 has some calcification hence is strengthened. The hypertrophic zone, however, is vulnerable to shearing forces, hence this is the area where physeal injuries occur. Fortunately there is a separate blood supply to the epiphysis (from vessels within the joint) and the metaphysis (from vessels of the periosteum and nutrient vessel), so physeal injuries rarely cause avascular necrosis apart from in the hip (see hip cases in Chapter 7).

Buckle of metaphysis

Lucent line transversing from metaphysis to physeal plate

# Case 5

Patient injured thumb in a rugby tackle, now painful thumb.

Describe the injury using Salter Harris classification.

Describe the five Salter Harris classifications, commenting on which areas of the bone they involve (for example, the metaphysis, and/or epiphysis).

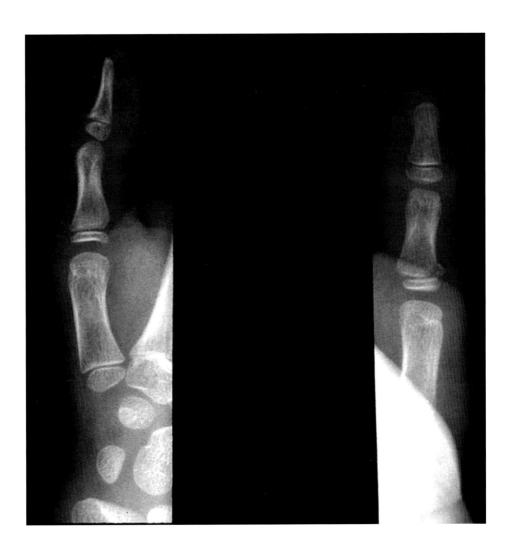

# Answer to Case 5

There is a fracture transversing the metaphysis of the proximal phalanx into the physeal plate, radial aspect; this was classified by Salter and Harris as a Salter Harris II.

Salter and Harris first described physeal injuries in 1963. Their classification system is extremely useful as it uses distinct radiographic patterns, and each injury has a clinical and prognostic significance. There are in fact up to nine types of Salter Harris fracture, but the most common are the five basic types shown below.

The classification system divides fractures into five types, depending upon the pattern of involvement of the adjacent bone; all involve the physeal plate (see Figure 2.1). The classification system also indicates prognosis – the lower the number the better the prognosis (hence Salter Harris I and II have a relatively good prognosis, whereas Salter Harris V fractures have a relatively poor prognosis).

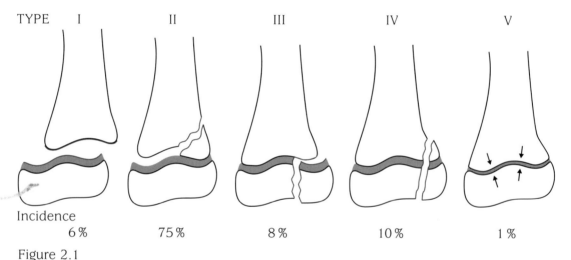

TYPE    I          II          III          IV          V

Incidence
    6%        75%        8%        10%        1%

Figure 2.1
**Salter Harris classification and incidence of occurrence**

As demonstrated in the figure, type I is a separation of the epiphysis and metaphysis at the physeal plate, type II is a separation at the physeal plate and a fracture of the metaphysis, type III is a fracture of the epiphysis, again involving physeal plate, type IV is a fracture transversing the physeal plate and involving the metaphysis and epiphysis, and type V is a compression of the physeal plate.

Eighty per cent of physeal plate injuries occur between the ages of 10 and 16 years of age, although Salter Harris I fractures are more common in the under 5s. The joint capsule and ligamentous structures are stronger than the physeal plate. Hence in an adult a certain trauma may result in ligamentous injury whereas the same trauma in a child will often result in a physeal plate injury.

**30**

The other four types of Salter Harris fractures are rare and often not mentioned, but for completeness are described.

- type VI – consists of an injury to the perichondral structures
- type VII – is an isolated injury to the epiphyseal plate
- type VIII – is an isolated injury to the metaphysis, with a potential injury related to endochondral ossification
- type IX – is an injury to the periosteum that may interfere with membranous growth.

## Case 6

Patient banged thumb on a piece of furniture, now painful and swollen.

Describe the radiographs.

What lies directly above the physeal plate of the distal phalanx of the hands and feet? What is the importance of this?

# Answer to Case 6

There is a widening of the physeal plate of the distal phalanx dorsally (demonstrated on the lateral radiograph). If you look closely there is a small flake of bone at the physeal plate which has come from the metaphysis, hence this is a Salter Harris type II injury. More commonly the mechanism of injury in this case results in a Salter Harris I of the distal phalanx.

Above the physeal plate of the distal phalanx is the nail bed, hence it may be an open injury resulting in osteomyelitis if no antibiotic cover is given.

Flake of bone from the metaphysis

Widening of physeal plate dorsally

Nail bed

Physeal plate

Stubbing toe or finger on furniture etc.

Figure 2.2

**Occult, open Salter Harris type I injury**

## Case 7

Patient fell injuring hand, bony tenderness mainly to little finger.

Describe the radiographs.

Is there an injury? If so, classify.

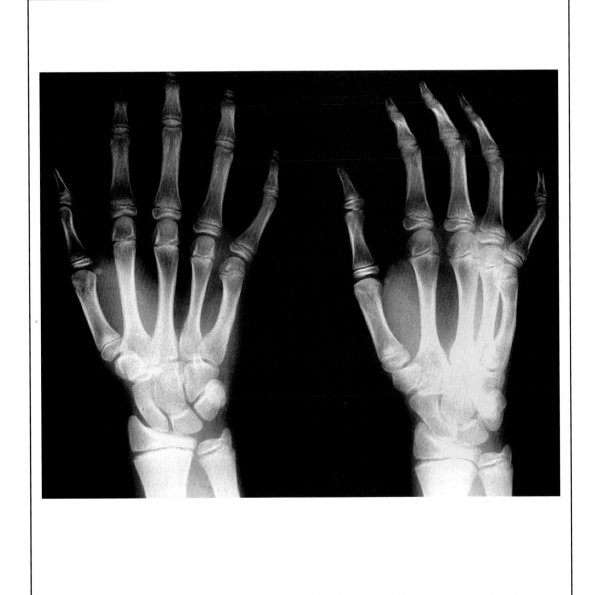

# Answer to Case 7

There is a break in the cortex and a lucent line at the metaphysis of the proximal phalanx, little finger ulnar aspect. The lucency travels from the metaphysis to the physeal plate; this is a Salter Harris II fracture. Physeal injuries are relatively common at the heads of metacarpals and bases of the proximal phalanges of the hands. This is an area of numerous physeal plates making it potentially a weak area in the hands. This type of injury is often difficult to visualise, requiring a magnification glass if using traditional radiography, or if computerised, magnifying on screen. They are best demonstrated on the oblique radiograph. In children, the proximal phalanx is involved in over 50 per cent of fractures of the phalanx.

Lucent line transversing metaphysis entering physeal plate = Salter Harris II; also small buckle of cortex here

# Case 8

Patient fell on outstretched hand.

Describe the injury.

Should another view be considered?

# Answer to Case 8

The posterior anterior view demonstrates a buckling of the cortex of the distal radius at the metaphysis. The lateral view clearly demonstrates a break in the cortex of the distal radius at the metaphysis; there is also slight dorsal angulation of the distal radius (instead of the normal volar angulation). On reviewing the lateral radiograph the fracture line probably enters the physeal plate, hence it is a Salter Harris II fracture (although difficult to visualise on this radiograph). Also there is widening of the volar aspect of the physeal plate (hence the physeal plate is involved). On a normal lateral radiograph the radius overlies the ulna which can sometimes make it difficult to view the dorsal metaphysis of the distal radius (as in this case). A radiograph with the hand slightly supinated will clear the dorsal radial border away from the ulna, demonstrating this area more clearly. Whether another view with the hand slightly supinated is carried out depends on whether it will alter patient management, local protocols, and the additional radiation dose to a young child.

When there is high suspicion of a fracture in this area, which is not demonstrated sufficiently on posterior anterior and lateral views, this additional oblique view should be considered in order to prevent missing a fracture.

Widening of volar aspect of physeal plate

Probable lucent line entering physeal plate

Break in cortex, dorsal aspect distal radial metaphysis

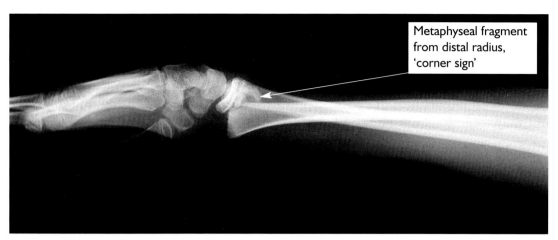

Metaphyseal fragment from distal radius, 'corner sign'

Figure 2.3

**Salter Harris II fracture of distal radius with displacement**

The most common site of epiphyseal injury is the distal radius, resulting from a fall on an outstretched hand. It may not be readily viewed on the posterior anterior radiograph. However on the lateral radiograph a fracture of the dorsal, distal radial metaphysis with widening of the volar physeal plate may be visualised (the 'corner sign'). Care is required in assessing this injury as the metaphyseal fragment may be undisplaced, due to the relative strength of the surrounding ligaments returning the metaphyseal fragment to its normal place when the force is removed. If the patient falls supinating their hand against their wrist then the metaphyseal fragment will be on the volar aspect of the radius, with widening of the dorsal aspect of the physeal plate (a Smith's type fracture in an adult).

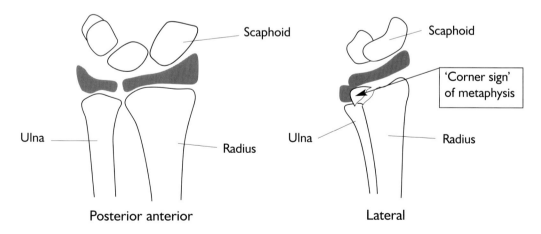

Scaphoid

Scaphoid

'Corner sign' of metaphysis

Ulna

Radius

Ulna

Radius

Posterior anterior

Lateral

Figure 2.4

**Salter Harris II fracture of the distal radius from a fall on outstretched hand**

# Case 9

Patient hit a wall with fist, now pain in fifth metacarpal (little finger metacarpal).

Describe the radiographs.

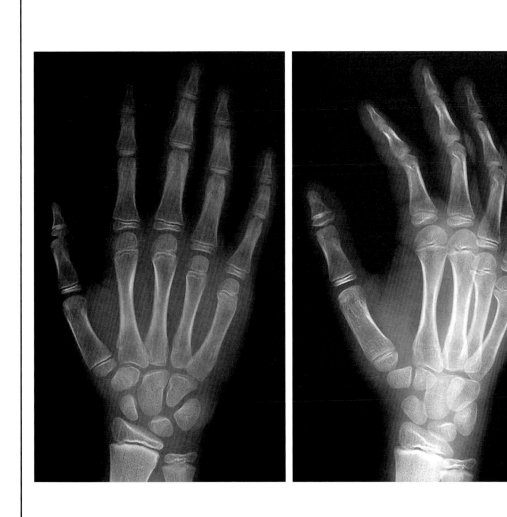

# Answer to Case 9

The posterior anterior view demonstrates a small buckle in the cortex of the fifth metacarpal (little finger) at the metaphysis. Often paediatric fractures are subtle, and it is useful to review many normal radiographs of each area so that it is easier to notice subtle buckles when they occur. In this case the oblique radiograph readily demonstrates the fracture. There is a break in the cortex of the dorsal aspect of the metaphysis of the fifth metatarsal (little finger); this is a greenstick fracture. New thinking suggests that instead of the fifth metacarpal we call it the little finger metacarpal, etc., to avoid confusion.

This buckle fracture in children would, in an adult, become a fracture of the neck of the fifth metacarpal (little finger metacarpal), commonly known as the 'boxer's fracture'.

Small buckle in cortex

# Case 10

Patient fell in games at school, painful deformed finger.

Describe the radiographs, and classify.

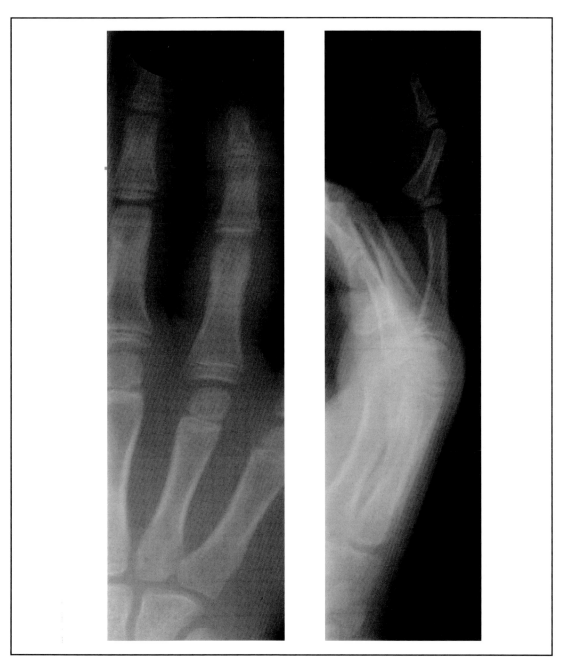

# Answer to Case 10

The posterior anterior view does not demonstrate the injury, which highlights the necessity of always reviewing two radiographic projections of the affected area at right angles to each other. The lateral view readily demonstrates the gross separation at the physeal plate, of the middle phalanx with volar displacement of the metaphysis. Two fragments of bone are present at the physeal area, one at the volar aspect, the other dorsal. These fragments of bone are probably from the metaphysis, hence this is a Salter Harris type II injury.

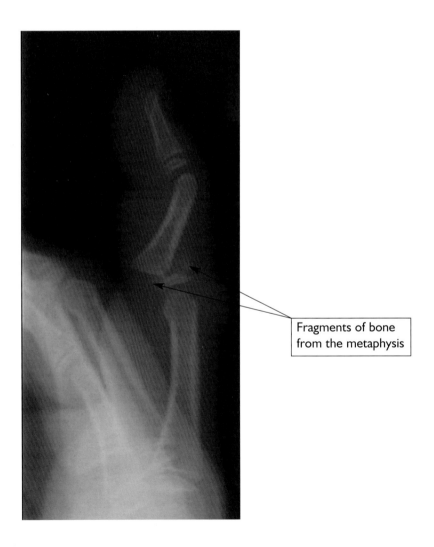

Fragments of bone from the metaphysis

# Case 11

Patient hyperextended finger in netball. Now painful finger and appears deformed.

Describe the radiographs.

Is there an injury?

Describe a common injury to the finger from hyperextension.

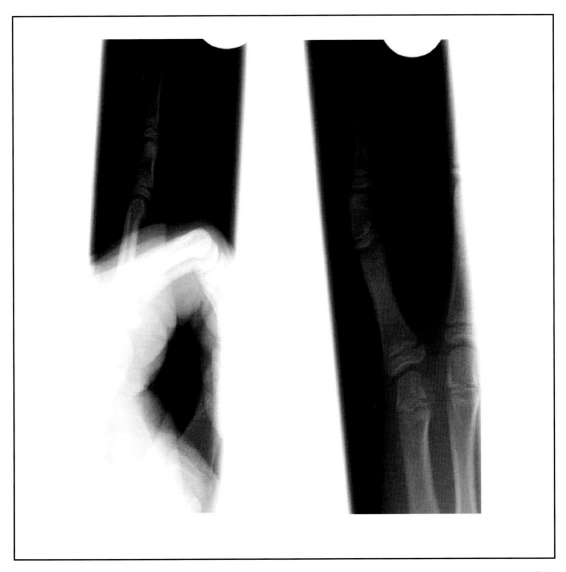

# Answer to Case 11

The patient has a shortened middle phalanx with what appears to be an angulated, accessory physeal plate distally, which results in the finger being angulated. This is clinodactyly of the fifth finger (Keats has a similar example in his book of normal variants). The clinician, on discussion with the child and mother, came to the conclusion that the finger was no more angulated than normal, plus the fifth finger on the other hand was the same. Be careful when reviewing paediatric hand radiographs as they can have accessory ossification centres and false ossification centres (particularly at the base of the metacarpals).

No injury was seen on the radiographs. A common injury from hyperextension of the finger is an avulsion of the volar aspect of the middle phalanx, a volar plate type avulsion.

Clinodactyly is a shortened middle phalanx (which may be angulated as in this case), whereas Kirner's anomaly is a shortened distal phalanx.

# Case 12

Patient fell on outstretched hand, now painful wrist.

Describe the radiographs.

# Answer to Case 12

On the anterior posterior radiograph a small buckle of the distal radius is visible. Also demonstrated is a buckle (torus) type fracture of the distal ulna. The lateral view demonstrates the torus fracture of the distal radius on the dorsal aspect; there is also dorsal angulation of the distal radius. Remember the distal radius is normally angulated volarly (10 to 15 degrees), and ulnarly (17 degrees) – alteration in this is a clue to injury. The torus fracture of the distal ulna is also demonstrated on the lateral view (remember to look through the radius to the ulnar on the lateral).

Torus fracture of the radius

Torus fracture of distal ulna

Dorsally angulated distal radius

Torus fracture of distal radius

Torus fracture of distal ulna

## Case 13

Patient fell from bike, injuring hand.

Describe and classify the injury.

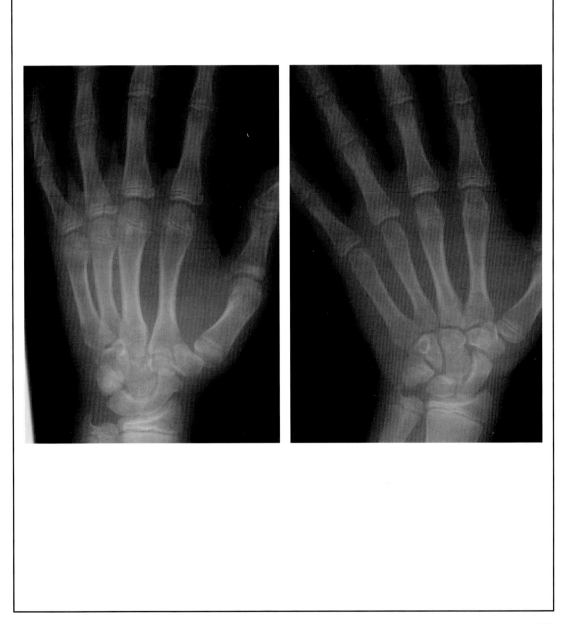

## Answer to Case 13

There is a vertical lucent line through the epiphysis of the proximal phalanx of the ring finger, with widening of the physeal plate, radial aspect. This is a Salter Harris type III injury. However on closer inspection of the oblique view (this type of injury is frequently more clearly demonstrated on the oblique view), a small fragment of the metaphysis, radial aspect of proximal phalanx is noted, hence this would make it a Salter Harris type IV injury.

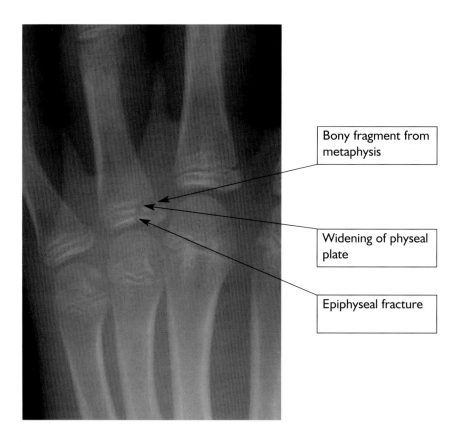

Bony fragment from metaphysis

Widening of physeal plate

Epiphyseal fracture

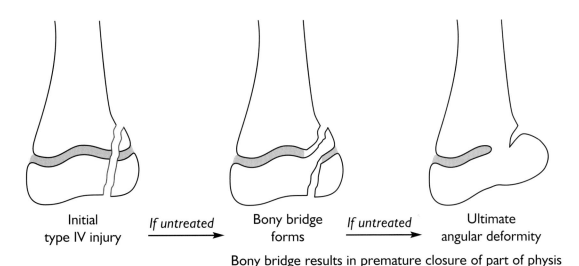

Initial type IV injury → *If untreated* → Bony bridge forms → *If untreated* → Ultimate angular deformity

Bony bridge results in premature closure of part of physis

Figure 2.5
**Growth disturbance in Salter Harris type IV injuries**

A problem with Salter Harris type IV injuries is that callus formation may occur across the physeal plate leading to premature closure of part of the physeal plate, resulting in an angular deformity of that bone at the joint. It is therefore imperative that Salter Harris type IV injuries are radiographically visualised and accurately reported to ensure correct management. Salter Harris type IV injuries are normally caused by a vertical splitting force. Even with careful management growth arrest and joint deformities are possible.

# Case 14

Patient hyperextended finger whilst playing netball.

Describe the radiographs.

If an adult had the same mechanism of injury, what type of injury would you be looking for?

## Answer to Case 14

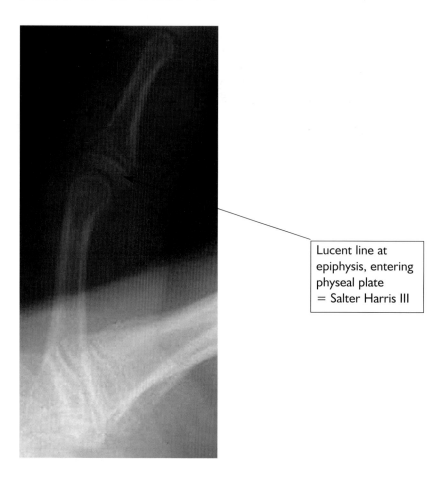

Lucent line at
epiphysis, entering
physeal plate
= Salter Harris III

There is a lucent line volar aspect of epiphysis of middle phalanx entering into the physeal plate, hence it is Salter Harris type III injury, involving about a third of the articular surface. Injuries involving more than a third of the articular surface often need more careful management to prevent early arthritis.

If an adult hyperextended their finger the most likely injury would be an avulsion of the volar aspect of the middle phalanx at the proximal interphalangeal joint (volar plate avulsion). This is due to the fact that in adolescence the physeal plate is much weaker than the ligaments or bone, hence with the same mechanism of injury an adult will receive a ligament or bony injury, whereas an adolescent will have a physeal injury (often involving nearby bone as well – as in this case).

# Case 15

Patient fell during games at school palmer flexing hand, now pain in wrist.

Describe the radiographs.

# Answer to Case 15

There is torus type fracture of the distal radius, demonstrated on the lateral view on the volar aspect, due to compression of the trabeculae (if this had been an adult it would have resulted in a Smith's type fracture). If the patient had fallen on their outstretched hand the torus fracture would have been on the dorsal aspect of the distal radius (in an adult this would have resulted in a Colles fracture).

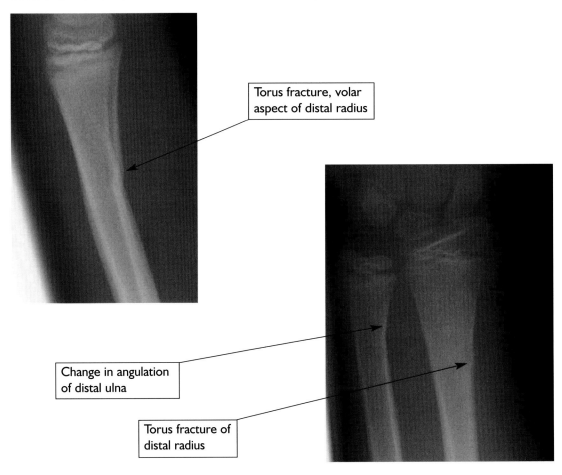

Torus fracture, volar aspect of distal radius

Change in angulation of distal ulna

Torus fracture of distal radius

The posterior anterior view demonstrates the torus fracture of the distal radius, but also demonstrates a sharp angulation of the distal ulna cortex, lateral aspect instead of the normal smooth curvature, slightly more distal than the radial fracture. This is a buckle type fracture of the distal ulna. Torus/buckle fractures are often very subtle, hence it is useful to review many normal paediatric radiographs in order to better appreciate subtle changes in alignment (see Case 60).

# 3.

# Elbow and forearm trauma

# Case 16

Patient fell onto elbow, now not using arm, bony tenderness at elbow area.

Describe the radiograph.

Is there a joint effusion?

What line is useful in assessing this type of injury in children?

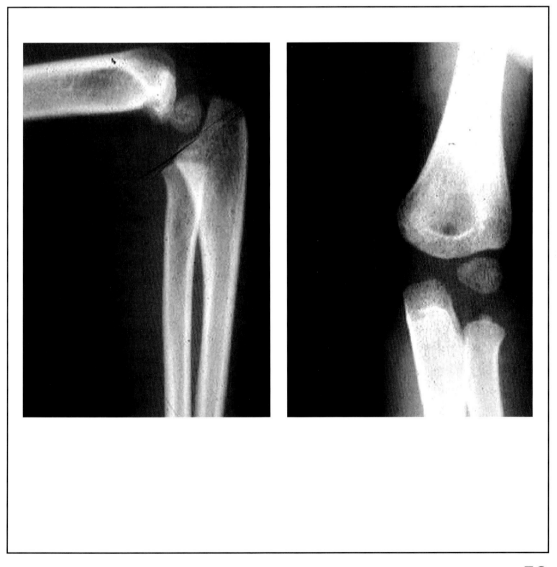

# Answer to Case 16

There is a supracondylar fracture. A lucent line and a break in the cortex can be seen at the volar aspect of the distal humeral metaphysis, and the medial epicondyle.

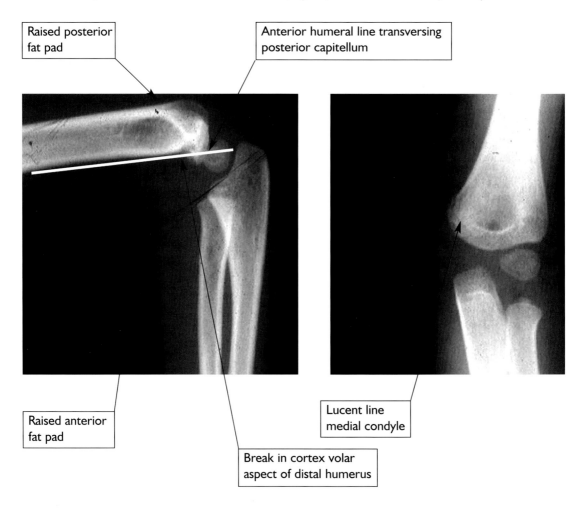

Raised posterior fat pad

Anterior humeral line transversing posterior capitellum

Raised anterior fat pad

Lucent line medial condyle

Break in cortex volar aspect of distal humerus

Sixty per cent of elbow fractures in children are supracondylar fractures. The main mechanism of injury is a fall onto an outstretched hand, although one per cent are caused by a direct fall onto the olecranon. The injury may result in cubitus varus or valgus. Most supracondylar fractures have posterior displacement of the condyles and an abnormal anterior humeral line. The injury may be occult. The main clues to injury are a positive fat pad sign (a joint effusion) and the anterior humeral line not passing through the anterior part of the middle third of the capitellum.

A thin layer of fat lies between the synovial and fibrous layers of both the anterior and posterior aspects of the elbow joint capsule. The two anterior fat pads lie in front of the coronoid fossa and radial fossa of the distal humerus, frequently merged anatomically, and can be seen on the radiograph as a straight lucency making an angle of 30 degrees. The posterior fat pad lies in the intercondylar depression of the posterior surface of the humerus and is not normally demonstrated radiographically. With a small joint effusion an abnormal convex or elevated ('sail sign') anterior fat pad may be seen. With a larger joint effusion the posterior fat pad will also be demonstrated on the lateral radiograph. Remember, though, that if the injury has caused a lot of soft tissue damage and the joint capsule is torn there will be no joint effusion demonstrated radiographically, as the fluid will flow away from the joint.

This case demonstrates a raised anterior fat pad, and posterior fat pad – there is a joint effusion.

Figure 3.1
**Anterior humeral line**

The most useful line for demonstrating a supracondylar fracture is the anterior humeral line. If you draw a line along the anterior border of the humerus, on a true lateral radiograph it should bisect the anterior part of the middle third of the capitellum. In this case the anterior humeral line bisects the posterior third of the capitellum which, along with the positive fat pad signs, is indicative of a supracondylar fracture, even if a fracture line cannot be seen. A patient with a positive fat pad sign and an anterior humeral line *not* transversing the correct part of the capitellum, should be treated as a supracondylar fracture, and re-x-rayed 10 to 14 days later, when often the fracture line is visible as bone is reabsorbed along the fracture line. Furthermore, by day 14 an early healing response should be seen in the form of a periosteal reaction.

Remember the fracture may not be complete; it may be a torus, greenstick or even bow fracture.

In this case, the anterior humeral line passes through the posterior capitellum, indicating anterior displacement of the capitellum (a fall on the point of the elbow). It is more usual for the capitellum to be displaced posteriorly in supracondylar or lateral condylar fractures, in which case the anterior humeral line passes anterior to the middle third of the capitellum – as in Case 17 (a fall on outstretched hand).

It is useful at this stage to review the anatomy of the elbow in children. The elbow is made up of three epiphyses – the trochlea, capitellum and proximal radius; and three apophyses – the olecranon, medial and lateral epicondyle.

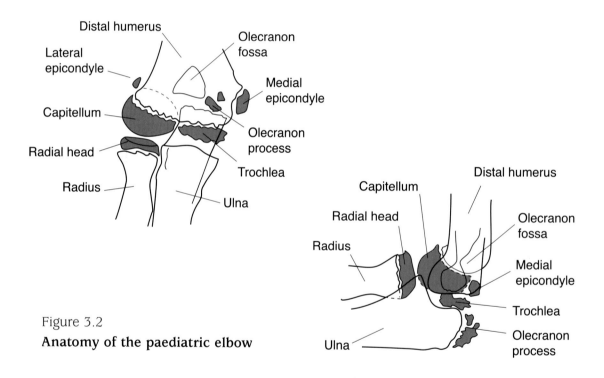

Figure 3.2
**Anatomy of the paediatric elbow**

As can be seen in the diagram both the olecranon process and trochlea can be quite fragmented, and should not be mistaken as a fracture. The medial epicondyle on the lateral radiograph can sometimes lie quite posteriorly, but should not lie within the joint (see Case 21).

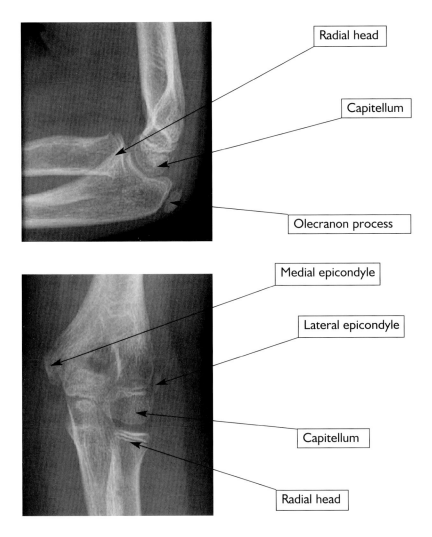

Figure 3.3
**Epiphyses and apophyses of the elbow joint**

**Epiphyses**

● Capitellum

● Radial head

● Trochlea

**Apophyses**

● Lateral epicondyle (origin: common forearm extensor muscles origin)

● Medial epicondyle (origin: common forearm flexor muscle origin)

● Olecranon (insertion: triceps brachii)

# Case 17

Patient fell on outstretched hand, not using elbow.

Describe the radiographs.

Is there a joint effusion?

Is the anterior humeral line within normal limits?

Is the olecranon normal?

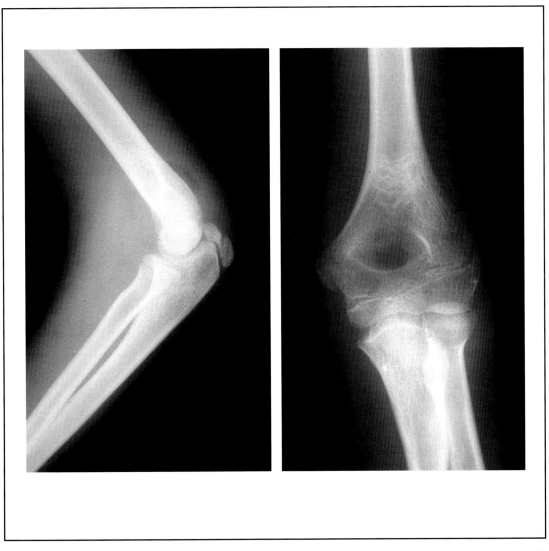

# Answer to Case 17

There is a lucent line entering the medial/superior olecranon notch, which is probably a supracondylar fracture. There are positive anterior and posterior fat pads, hence there is a joint effusion. The anterior humeral line traverses the anterior capitellum indicative of a supracondylar fracture. The olecranon process is normal.

The elbow in children is made up of both epiphyses and apophyses (see Figure 3.3). An epiphysis is for longitudinal growth of a bone and is within a joint, an apophysis does not contribute to longitudinal growth of the bone and is not within a joint. Multicentric ossification of these secondary centres may erroneously suggest fragmentation or fracture; the fragmented olecranon process in this case is normal.

Raised posterior fat pad

Raised anterior fat pad

Anterior humeral line traversing anterior capitellum

The original report for this patient noted the joint effusion and abnormal anterior humeral, commenting that they were indicative of a supracondylar fracture. Hence the patient was treated as a supracondylar fracture and re-x-rayed 14 days later. Now you can see the fracture line (although it was visible on the initial radiographs), and a periosteal reaction along the anterior/medial border of the distal humerus, as it starts to heal.

Periosteal
reaction

Fracture
line

# Case 18

Patient fell on outstretched hand. Describe the radiographs (below and on page 68 opposite).

Is there a joint effusion?

Is this a true lateral view?

Is the bony protuberance of the anterior humerus normal? What is it called? Does it have any significance

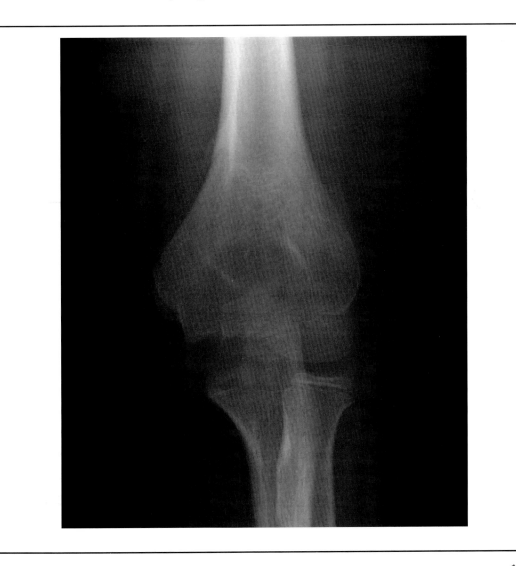

# Answer to Case 18

There is a lucent line traversing the superior aspect of the metaphysis of the proximal radius, entering the physeal plate. This is a Salter Harris type II injury. The lateral radiograph is not a true lateral which can make it difficult in the assessment of raised fat pads and affect the anterior humeral line (although in this age group it can be extremely difficult to achieve high-quality radiographs). The lateral radiograph demonstrates a triangular anterior fat pad, which is somewhat raised, but would be more readily demonstrated on a true lateral; posteriorly a fat pad can be visualised overlaid by bone (this would be more readily appreciated on a true lateral). The fracture is radiographically demonstrated and, due to the patient's age, a repeat true lateral radiograph is not required – it would not alter patient management and would increase the child's radiation dose.

The radiograph also demonstrates a bony protuberance on the anterior, medial border of the distal humerus – a supracondylar spur. The supracondylar spur can lie close to the site of the supracondylar fracture, therefore a fracture of the spur may compress or injure either the brachial artery or median nerve.

Supracondylar spur

Posterior fat pad overlaid by bone

Raised anterior fat pad

Salter Harris II fracture

## Case 19

Patient fell onto arm yesterday, now not using arm and crying on movement.

X-ray request asked for whole arm to be x-rayed.

Describe the radiograph.

## Answer to Case 19

Unfortunately only one radiograph is available. Depending on the age and size of the child we should always obtain separate arm and forearm radiographs, otherwise subtle fractures may be missed. This radiograph demonstrates a transverse fracture of the radial head, an unusual injury in this age group (see Case 1). This case reminds us that the associations between injury type and age groups (see p. 21) are just guidelines to help in radiological diagnosis.

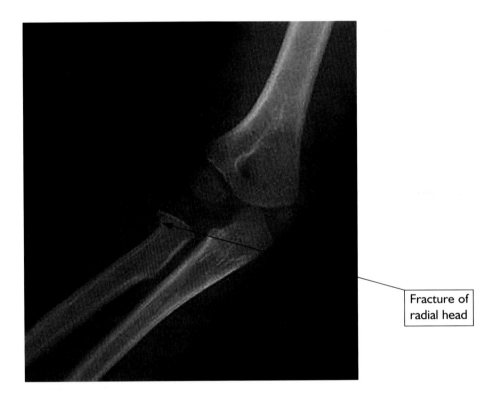

Fracture of radial head

# Case 20

Patient fell onto arm, now painful whole length of forearm, with limited movement.

Describe the radiographs.

Would another view be helpful?

# Answer to Case 20

A positive anterior fat pad can be seen at the elbow and there appears to be a buckle fracture of the volar aspect of the radial head. This demonstrates the importance of looking carefully at all aspects of the radiograph, particularly the edges. An anterior posterior radiograph of the elbow would be useful; because the radiograph was taken to demonstrate the forearm, an oblique presentation of the elbow joint has been obtained. The anterior posterior view demonstrates the fracture and steep radial angulation (about 45 degrees) of the metaphysis.

Raised anterior fat pad

Buckle type fracture of radial proximal metaphysis

Fracture of radial metaphysis with angulation

# Case 21

Adolescent fell, injuring elbow; unsure of mechanism of injury.

Describe the radiograph.

What is the normal mechanism of injury for this type of trauma?

What complication can occur in this type of injury?

# Answer to Case 21

This is an older child, where the physeal plates have fused. There is an avulsion of the medial epicondyle. Ten per cent of elbow injuries in children are avulsions of the medial epicondyle. Mechanisms of injury are a fall on the outstretched hand, violent contraction of the flexor pronator muscle during the act of throwing (sometimes called 'little leaguer's elbow', in America), or dislocation of the elbow.

One of the complications that can occur is entrapment of the medial epicondyle (occurs in ten per cent of children) but this may go unrecognised, resulting in severe late disability. Valgus stress initially occurs at the time of injury with temporary widening of the elbow joint space medially. The avulsed epicondyle is drawn into the joint by traction from the attached flexor pronator muscle group, and the ulnar collateral ligament. When the force is released the joint is closed, entrapping the medial epicondyle. Prior to the appearance of all the epiphyses and apophyses the injury may go unrecognised as the avulsed epicondyle is mistaken for the trochlea. It is therefore important to know the ossification sequence of the elbow.

There are two memory aids, the most common being the acronym **CRITOL**.

- **C** apitellum – 1 year

- **R** adial head – 3 to 6 years

- **I** nternal (medial) epicondyle – 4 to 7 years

- **T** rochlea – 9 to 10 years

- **O** lecranon – 10 years

- **L** ateral epicondyle – 11 years

Hence the trochlea is never seen radiographically without also seeing the medial epicondyle.

An alternative for remembering the sequence of ossification of the elbow is Nelson's X mnemonic, as demonstrated in Figure 3.4.

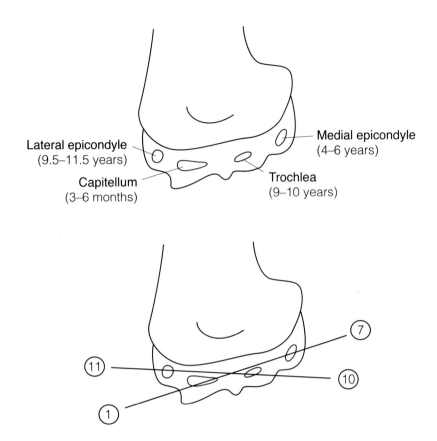

Figure 3.4
**Nelson's X mnemonic for sequence of ossification of the elbow – 1, 7, 10, 11 (years)**

Avulsions of the medial epicondyle may be subtle, and there are not always positive fat pads as a clue to injury, because the medial epicondyle is extracapsular in some patients. Also when associated with dislocation the joint capsule may be disrupted, allowing escape of joint fluids. The medial epicondyle may lie quite posteriorly on the lateral radiograph (see Case 16); it should not however project over the region of the capitellum or joint space. When reviewing a radiograph for avulsion of the medial epicondyle look for loss of parallelism between the epicondyle and adjacent metaphysis. The medial apophyseal centre should have a complete surrounding thin rim of sclerosis; with subtle malrotations subsequent to fracture this peripheral rim may be absent.

# Case 22

Patient fell injuring elbow, now painful, with limited movement.

Describe the radiographs.

Following this type of injury, what other area of the arm should be radiographically reviewed?

What is the name of the normal variant demonstrated?

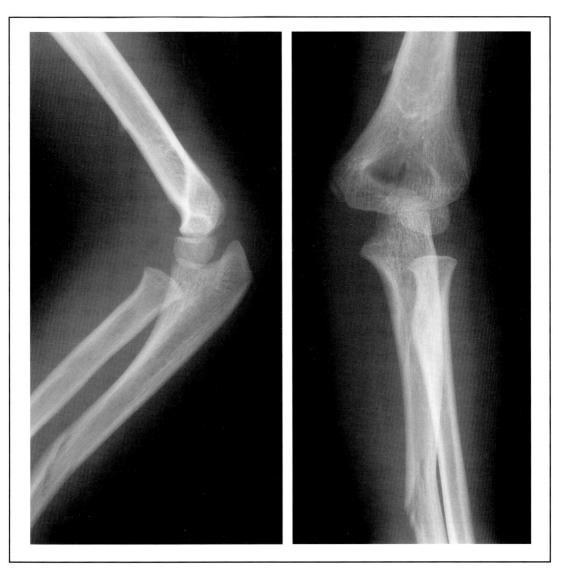

# Answer to Case 22

There is a greenstick type fracture of the mid third of the ulna. The radius and ulna are like a bony ring – if you identify a fracture of one then look for a fracture of the other or for a dislocation. The whole length of the radius and ulna including the elbow and wrist joints needs to be radiographed. There is no fracture of the radius in this case (demonstrated on the radiographs that follow). If only the ulna is fractured then look carefully at the radial head, and use the radiocapitellar line to check for dislocation (an ulnar shaft fracture in the presence of a dislocation is termed a Monteggia fracture dislocation). A line drawn along the long axis of the radius should bisect the capitellum (and is not dependent on radiographic position); if it does not then there is dislocation of the radial head.

It is possible to have an isolated fracture of the ulna or radius with no associated dislocation, commonly occuring following a direct blow. An isolated fracture of the ulna is frequently called a 'night stick' injury, occurring when the individual extends an arm up to protect themselves from attack from a 'stick'.

A fracture of the radius associated with dislocation at the radio–ulnar joint, is called a Galeazzi fracture dislocation. With a Monteggia fracture dislocation in an adult the fracture is often obvious, the dislocation of the radial head less so; in children the fracture is often less obvious, as it may be an incomplete fracture. There is no dislocation of the radial head in this case; it is not a Monteggia fracture dislocation.

The normal variant demonstrated in this case is a supracondylar spur (see Case 18).

Table 3.1 **Monteggia fracture dislocation in children**

| Type | Dislocation of radial head | Ulnar fracture | Radial fracture |
|---|---|---|---|
| I (most common) | Anterior | Proximal 1/3 of shaft, anterior angulation | |
| II | Posterior | Proximal 1/3 of shaft, posterior angulation | |
| III (second most common associated with radial neck injury) | Lateral | Metaphyseal (greenstick) | |
| IV | Anterior | Proximal 1/3 of shaft | Proximal radius |

Monteggia equivalent type fracture equals fracture of the proximal radius without radial head dislocation.

# Case 23

Patient fell whilst doing a handstand, now painful forearm.

Describe the radiographs.

What is the name for this type of injury?

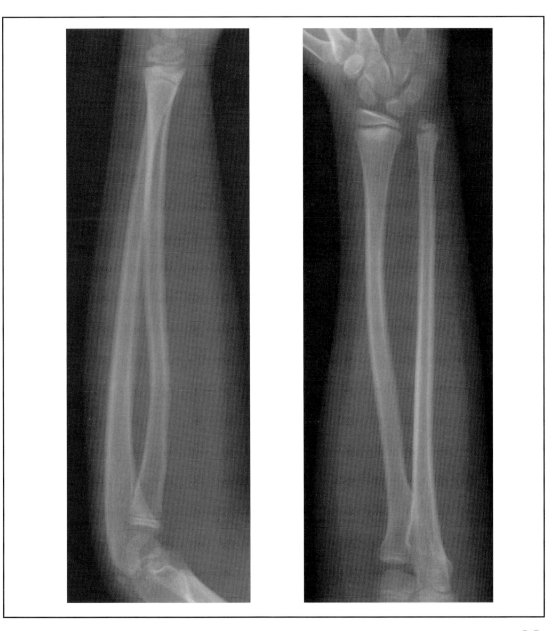

# Answer to Case 23

There is a greenstick fracture (a subtle break in cortex at the site of angulation) of the proximal radius. Distally there is loss of congruity at the radio–ulnar joint. This is called a Galeazzi fracture dislocation. As mentioned in Case 22 the forearm should be treated as a bony ring; if one fracture is identified, look for another or a dislocation. The ulna normally lies two millimetres proximal to the distal radius; remember that there are ulnar variances – both negative and positive variants. Ulnar negative variance is associated with Keinboch's disease (avascular necrosis of the lunate). Ulnar positive variance is associated with increased incidence of triangular fibrocartilage tears.

Figure 3.5

**Ulnar variance (true dorsipalmar radiograph required with no rotation)**
Normal range = 2.3 to 4.2 cm

# Case 24

Patient fell during games, unsure of mechanism of injury. All forearm painful, difficulty moving arm.

Describe the radiographs.

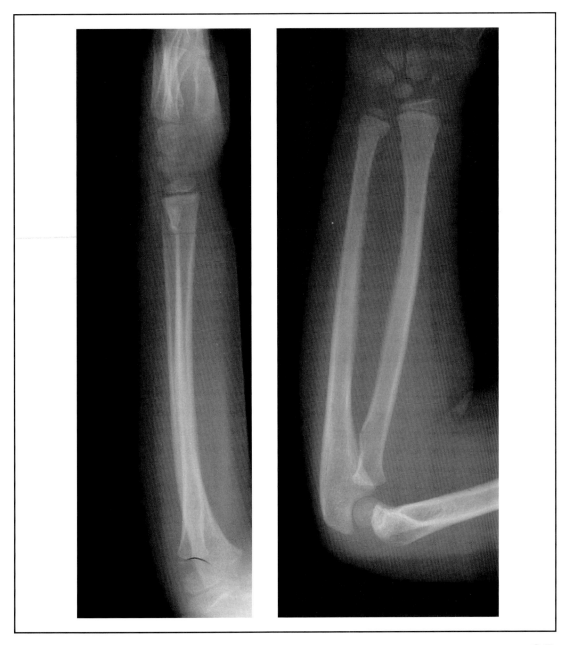

# Answer to Case 24

There is a torus fracture of the distal radius (remember always to look extra carefully at both joints on forearm radiographs). In adults a number of patients that have fracture of the distal radius also have fractures of the distal ulna; this is also the case in children, hence the distal ulna requires careful review. The anterior posterior radiograph demonstrates what appears to be a greenstick fracture of the distal ulna. On review of the lateral radiograph a completely separated fragment of the dorsal aspect of the distal ulna is demonstrated. Also demonstrated on the lateral view is the dorsal angulation of the distal radius (remember the distal radius is normally angulated volarly by 10 to 15 degrees).

# Case 25

Patient fell onto arm, painful forearm, unable to move arm.

Describe the radiographs.

What is this type of injury called?

## Answer to Case 25

The lateral radiograph demonstrates a torus fracture of the dorsal aspect of the distal radial metaphysis, a common injury from a fall on the outstretched hand. This case highlights the importance of looking carefully at all aspects of the forearm, particularly both joints.

# 4.

# Shoulder trauma

# Case 26

Patient fell directly onto shoulder, now painful clavicle on movement.

Describe the radiograph.

What are the main mechanisms of injury?

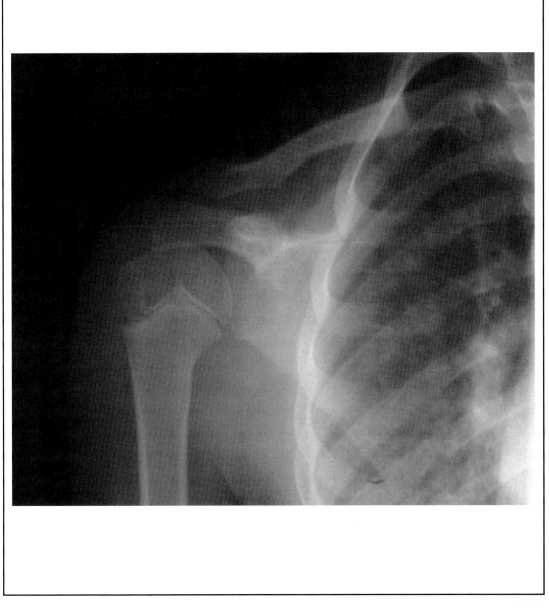

## Answer to Case 26

There is a fracture of the distal clavicle. A fracture of the clavicle is common injury in children. Fifty per cent of fractures of the clavicle occur in those under 10 years of age. 90 per cent of fractures of the clavicle are caused by a fall directly onto the shoulder. A direct blow or fall on the outstretched hand are less common mechanisms of injury. Around 80 per cent of fractures occur in the mid clavicle, 15 per cent to the distal clavicle and 5 per cent to the proximal clavicle.

Fractured clavicle

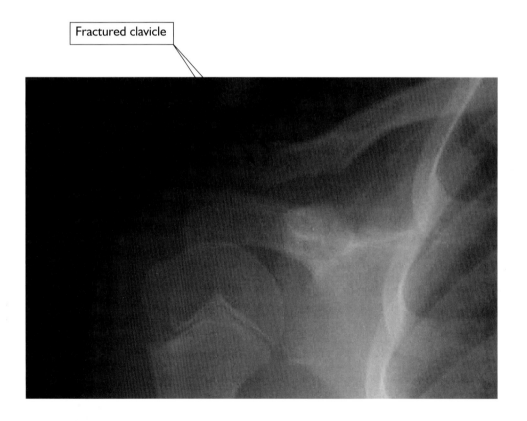

# Case 27

Patient fell onto shoulder, now painful at acromio–clavicular joint and length of clavicle.

Describe the radiograph.

Is there an injury?

# Answer to Case 27

There is no bony injury, or acromio–clavicular joint dislocation demonstrated on these radiographs. The non-alignment of the inferior surface of the acromion and clavicle is normal for a child, but in an adult would represent subluxation. The relative positions of the acromion and clavicle can not be assessed due to unossified cartilage. Acromio–clavicular joint subluxations are rare in children, the normal age range for this injury being 15 to 40 years. However, pseudo dislocation is possible.

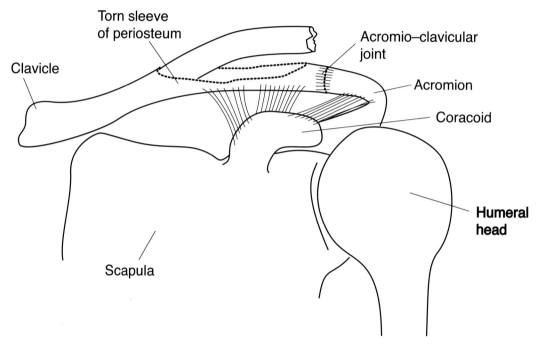

Figure 4.1
**Pseudo dislocation of the acromio–clavicular joint in a child**

Clinically and radiographically acromio–clavicular pseudo dislocation appears as a complete acromio–clavicular joint dislocation, but at surgery a torn periosteal sleeve is found with intact coraco–clavicular ligaments. If this injury remains untreated a Y-shaped clavicle results.

# Case 28

Patient fell directly onto shoulder, now unable to move arm, bony tenderness to clavicle.

Describe the radiograph.

At what age does the medial clavicular epiphysis ossify and fuse?

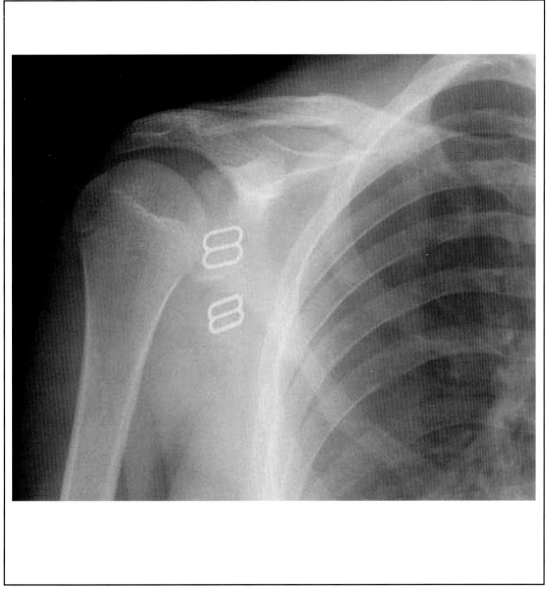

# Answer to Case 28

There is a fracture of the mid third of the clavicle (the most common area of the clavicle to fracture). Sometimes this type of fracture can be quite difficult to see as it is often superimposed radiographically over the spine of the scapula. Often when a clavicle fracture is clinically suspected, but not radiographically demonstrated, a cranially angulated radiograph of the clavicle is done (demonstrating it clear of the spine of the scapula).

Fracture of clavicle

Another case with a cranially angled view of the clavicle demonstrating a mid shaft fracture clear of the spine of scapula.

The medial clavicular epiphysis is the last to ossify, at 18 to 20 years of age, and is the last to fuse, at 25 to 26 years of age. Without this information it is easy to mistake a normal medial clavicle epiphysis as a fracture of the medial clavicle. Hence it is possible to have a Salter Harris I fracture of the medial clavicle up to 26 years of age.

## Case 29

Patient fell off slide injuring shoulder, now painful to move.

Describe the radiograph.

How many centres of ossification form the humeral head, and at what age do they appear?

# Answer to Case 29

There is a torus fracture of the proximal shaft of the humerus.

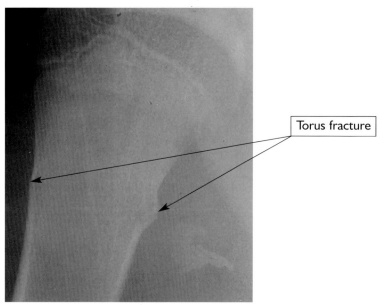

Torus fracture

The humeral head has three centres of ossification. The ossification centre for the humeral head appears first at 4 to 6 months of age, then the greater tubercle at 3 years of age, and the lesser tubercle at 5 years of age; they coalesce at 7 years of age. It is particularly important with children to know what is normal radiographic anatomy so that abnormal anatomy can be more readily identified. It is useful to have a text of normal radiographic anatomy at different ages at hand for the radiograph reporter. Below are three normal radiographs at different ages of the shoulder to give an idea of the normal radiographic anatomy, when the humeral head ossification centres appear.

*Left to right*
4–6 months to 3 years
3 to 5 years
5 years until fusion

Figure 4.2
**Normal shoulder radiographs in children**

# Case 30

Patient fell onto shoulder, bony tenderness to humeral head.

Describe the radiographs.

Classify the injury.

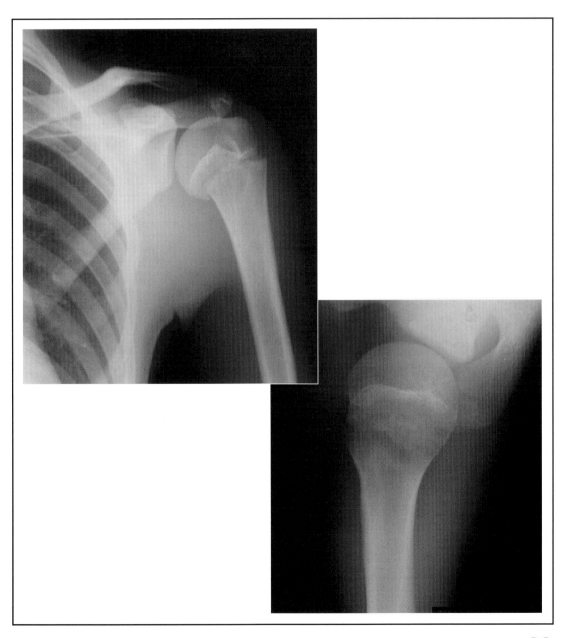

# Answer to Case 30

There is a separation of the humeral head physeal plate lateral aspect (anteroposterior radiograph), involving the metaphysis medially (axial radiograph); this is a Salter Harris type II injury. There is lateral displacement of the diaphysis (remember always describe movement of the distal part, not the proximal part).

The proximal humeral physeal plate on the anterior posterior view in external rotation is shaped like an inverted V or chevron. Below shows a normal humeral physeal plate – care is needed not to mistake the physeal plate for a fracture. The proximal humeral epiphysis is responsible for 80 per cent of growth of the humerus. Physeal separation is rare, but most commonly occurs from 10 to 15 years of age. Salter Harris I injuries are more common in the under 10s, whereas Salter Harris II are more common in the 10–15 age group.

**Normal physeal plate of humerus**

Normal double line of physis (if you follow one round it will join up with the other) – not to be mistaken as a fracture

# Case 31

Patient fell hitting proximal humerus against a shelf, now extremely painful.

Describe the radiograph.

Name the pathology.

# Answer to Case 31

There is a fracture through a simple bone cyst in the proximal humeral diaphysis. No lateral radiograph was available.

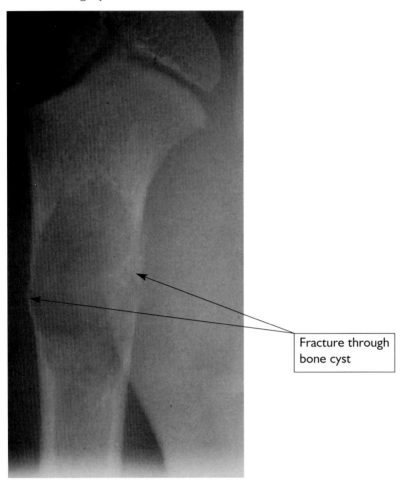

Fracture through bone cyst

This is a benign fluid-filled bone lesion of children (sometimes called a unicameral bone cyst). These cysts are often central geographic lesions, often in the metaphysis, but may migrate to the diaphysis (as in this case) as the skeleton matures. Proximal humerus is the most common site (50 per cent), although sometimes they occur in the proximal femur (20 per cent). Occasionally they may heal spontaneously following fracture.

# Case 32

Fourteen-year-old patient fell onto shoulder, painful acromion.

Describe the radiograph.

At what age do the coracoid and acromion apophyses fuse?

## Answer to Case 32

There is no bony injury. The lucency seen crossing the lateral tip of the acromion is an apophysis. If you look carefully the coracoid apophysis can also be seen. The scapula arises from several ossification centres that can easily be mistaken for fractures. Small slivers of ossification centres on the superior aspect of coracoid and the acromion can easily be mistaken for avulsion fractures. The coracoid and acromion apophyses fuse at about 15 years of age; the apophysis of the inferior border of the scapula fuses at about 20 years of age.

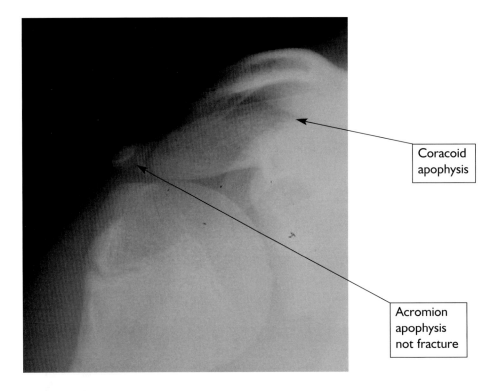

Coracoid apophysis

Acromion apophysis not fracture

## Case 33

Patient fell off swing, limited movement in shoulder.

Describe the radiographs.

Where are the physeal plate, metaphysis and diaphysis of the humerus?

Where are the glenoid, acromion and coracoid on the axial view?

# Answer to Case 33

There is a fracture of the surgical neck of the humerus. When reviewing children's shoulder radiographs take care not to mistake the physeal plate of the humerus for a fracture. Often two physeal lines can be seen (as shown below), but if you trace one of the physeal lines round it should meet up with the other physeal line (see Case 30). The epiphysis, metaphysis and diaphysis are shown in the anterior posterior radiograph.

**Anterior posterior radiograph**

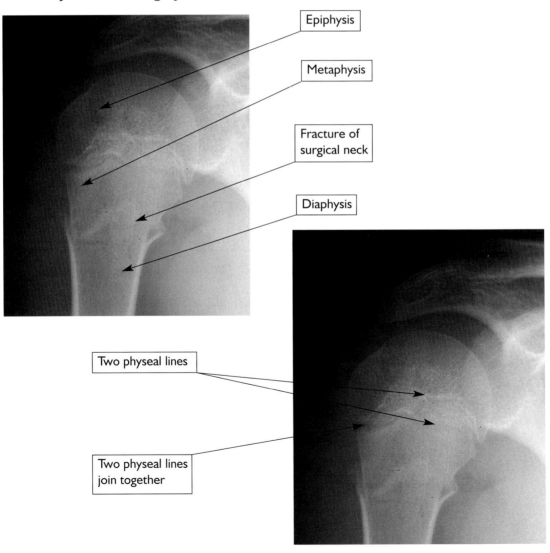

Epiphysis

Metaphysis

Fracture of surgical neck

Diaphysis

Two physeal lines

Two physeal lines join together

The acromion, glenoid fossa and coracoid are seen in the axial view.

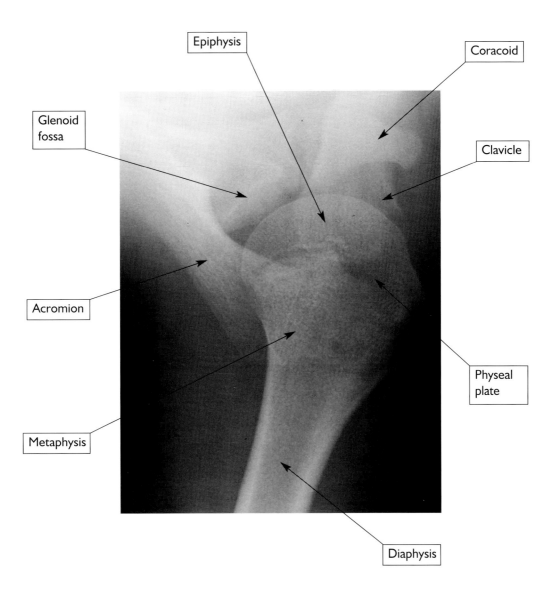

## Case 34

Patient fell from bike onto shoulder, now limited movement.

Describe the radiographs.

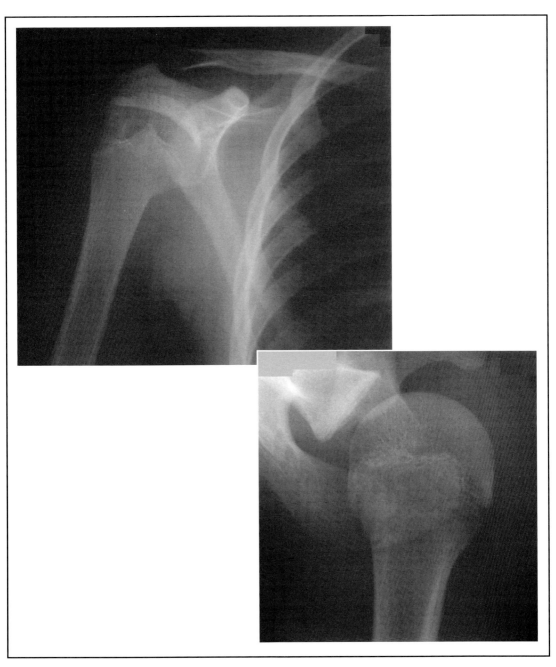

# Answer to Case 34

There is a sudden angulation at the medial aspect of the surgical neck of the humerus (demonstrated on the anterior posterior view), which is indicative of a fracture. The axial view clearly demonstrates a break in the cortex which appears to cross the shaft of the bone. This lucent line is not a physeal plate but a fracture (it does not join up with the physeal line seen proximal to it; see Cases 30 and 33).

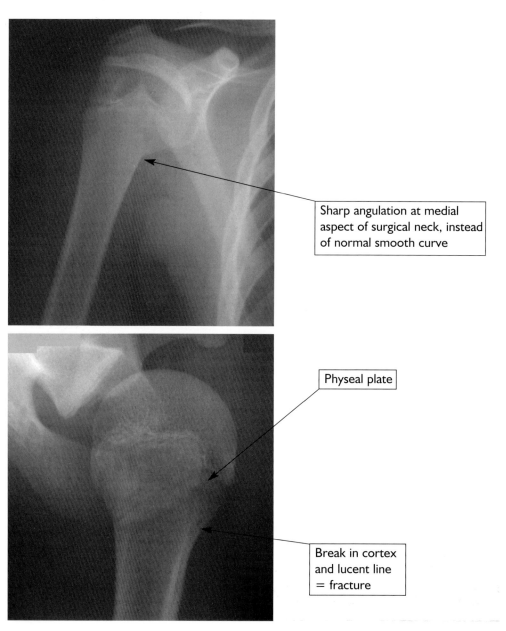

Sharp angulation at medial aspect of surgical neck, instead of normal smooth curve

Physeal plate

Break in cortex and lucent line = fracture

# Case 35

Patient suffered from previous dislocations and subluxations of the shoulder. Today painful shoulder following playing football.

Describe the radiographs.

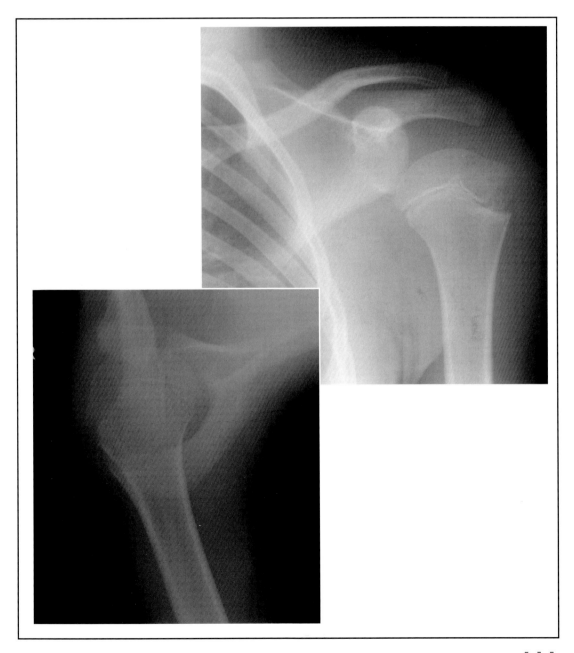

# Answer to Case 35

The anterior posterior radiograph demonstrates that the humeral head has moved inferiorly with regards to the glenoid. The axial view demonstrates that the articular surface of the humeral head is no longer in apposition with the glenoid – it is an anterior dislocation of the humeral head. Dislocations are relatively rare in children, but as with adults always require two projections (an anterior posterior view and an axial, or Y view or modified axial) to assess whether there is a dislocation.

**Modified axial view**

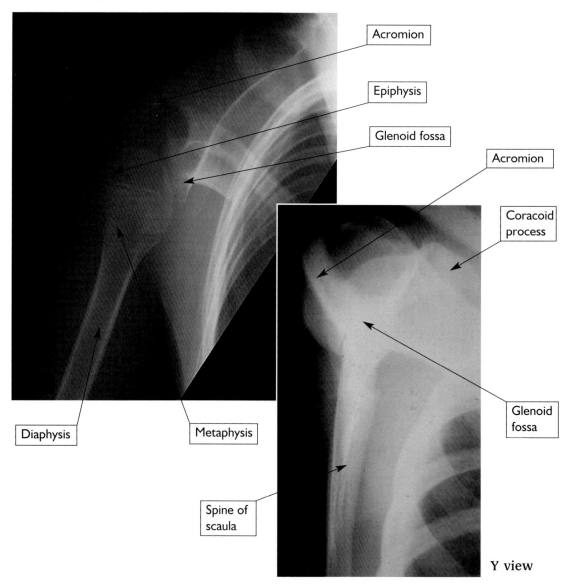

Acromion

Epiphysis

Glenoid fossa

Acromion

Coracoid process

Glenoid fossa

Diaphysis

Metaphysis

Spine of scaula

Y view

# 5.

# Ankle and foot trauma

# Case 36

Patient fell off skateboard, injuring ankle.

Describe the radiographs.

Classify the injury.

Comment on the age that the ankle ossification centres appear.

# Answer to Case 36

There is an oblique fracture of the distal tibia entering the physeal plate (resulting in widening of the physeal plate medially); there is also a small fragment of bone in the medial physeal plate. Any fracture that involves the physeal plate can be classified using the Salter Harris classification system. This is a Salter Harris type II injury (see p. 30). There is also a torus injury of the distal fibula diaphysis.

## Ossification centres of the ankle joint

- 6 months – distal tibial epiphysis appears

- 18 months – distal fibular epiphysis appears

- 5 years – epiphysis same width as metaphysis

- 10 years – malleoli well developed

- 12–13 years – assume adult appearance, fusion begins

- 14 years – tibia fused (girls), fibula 1 year later (boys fuse later)

On the next page are some ankle radiographs at various developmental stages, to assist when differentiating the normal ankle radiograph from the abnormal – as mentioned previously it is vital to have readily available texts of normal development and variants.

Normal epiphysis at 1 year

Normal epiphysis at 4 years

Normal epiphysis at 12 years

# Case 37

Patient fell twisting ankle, now bony tenderness of distal tibia and fibula.

Describe the radiographs.

Discuss the use of additional radiographs in this patient.

## Answer to Case 37

There is an oblique lucent line visualised on the lateral radiograph, which is a fracture. The lucent line is not visible on the anterior-posterior radiograph. It is difficult to assess on these radiographs whether this fracture is of the tibia or fibula, although the lucent line appears to stop at the physeal plate of the tibia (remember that the distal fibular physis should lie at the level of the ankle joint), indicating a fracture of the tibia – a Salter Harris II.

Management of the patient may differ according to whether the fibula or tibia is fractured. If the radiological conclusion of which bone was fractured in this case had not correlated with clinical findings, then oblique radiographs of the ankle would have been helpful. An anterior-posterior radiograph taken 10 days later demonstrates periosteal reaction (callus formation) along the tibial shaft, confirming it was a fracture of the tibia. This radiograph also demonstrates a vertical lucent line in the tibial epiphysis (not visualised previously). This, combined with the fracture demonstrated on the previous lateral, is a triplane fracture (see Case 41).

Callus formation

Lucent line in epiphysis

## Case 38

Patient playing games at school, fell and twisted ankle.

Describe the radiographs, and classify any injury.

## Answer to Case 38

There is a lucent line on the dorsal aspect of distal tibial metaphysis entering the physeal plate. This is a Salter Harris II injury. Injuries involving the physeal plate are just as common in the foot and ankle as other parts of the body.

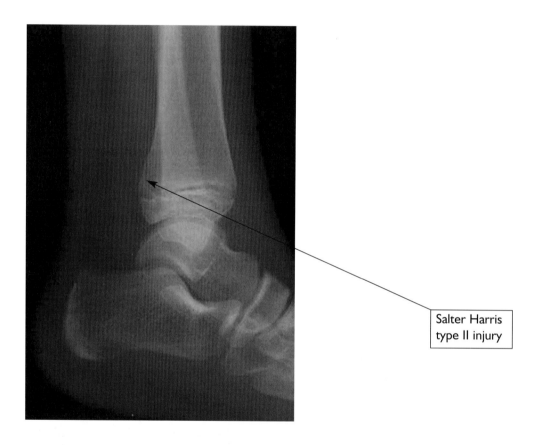

Salter Harris
type II injury

## Case 39

Patient involved in a rugby tackle, painful ankle ever since. Unsure of mechanism of injury.

Describe the radiographs and classify any injury.

## Answer to Case 39

There is a vertical lucent line on the medial aspect of the distal tibia epiphysis, which probably enters the physeal plate. This is a Salter Harris type III injury. There is a widening of the medial joint space. If this was a true mortice view this would be indicative of lateral talar shift, however it is not. Talar shift cannot be assessed on this radiograph (the leg is externally rotated too much). A repeat radiograph with the leg more internally rotated to obtain a true mortice view would be required to assess talar shift.

Salter Harris
type III injury

## Case 40

Patient twisted ankle, now painful distal fibula.

Describe the radiographs.

Would another view be helpful?

# Answer to Case 40

There appears to be a small bony fragment within the posterior ankle joint space, possibly from the fibula. There is also a large joint effusion at the ankle joint. Clinical history suggests injury of the distal fibula. A lateral oblique view of the ankle would demonstrate the distal fibula more clearly. The oblique view demonstrates a Salter Harris II fracture of the distal fibula.

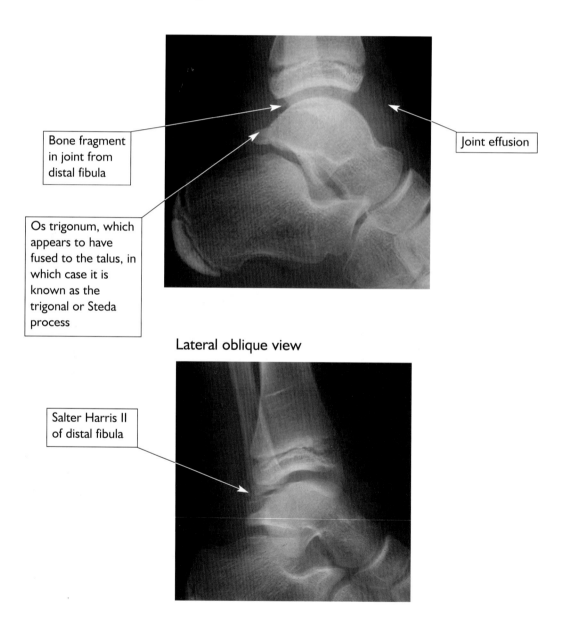

Bone fragment in joint from distal fibula

Joint effusion

Os trigonum, which appears to have fused to the talus, in which case it is known as the trigonal or Steda process

**Lateral oblique view**

Salter Harris II of distal fibula

## Case 41

Patient fell off bicycle, ankle caught in pedals, now painful and swollen.

Describe the radiographs.

What is the name for this type of injury?

Which part of the distal tibial physeal plate is the last to fuse?

Approximately at what age does this occur?

How does this affect trauma to the ankle joint?

# Answer to Case 41

If you review the anterior posterior view there is a vertical lucent line that traverses the epiphysis and there is widening of the lateral tibial physeal plate. If this was classified by Salter Harris it would be a Salter Harris III. At 12.5 years of age the distal tibia physeal plate starts to fuse; the lateral aspect is the last to fuse at about 14 years of age (Figure 5.1); this results in this being a weak area. Remember the physeal plate is weaker than the surrounding ligaments. In an adult following certain mechanisms of injury the ligaments of the distal tibio–fibula syndesmosis will be injured, but in an adolescent with a partially fused distal tibia the same mechanism of injury is more likely to result in a Tillaux fracture (a fracture of the lateral tibial epiphysis).

However if you look at the lateral radiograph then the lucent line can be seen crossing the epiphysis, but there also appears to be another lucent line crossing obliquely the dorsal aspect of the metaphysis. This case demonstrates a triplane fracture – a fracture that crosses three planes, vertically in the epiphysis, transversely in the physeal plate then changes direction again to cross caudally in the metaphysis (as shown in Figure 5.2). They can be divided into two-part injuries or three-part injuries and commonly occur as the distal tibia is fusing (see Figures 5.3, 5.4, 5.5). If you see what looks like a juvenile Tillaux fracture then look very carefully at the dorsal aspect of the distal tibia metaphysis to check that there is not another fracture line and that it is not a juvenile triplane fracture (Figure 5.3). Sometimes computerised axial tomography is useful to demonstrate the extent of injury in triplane fractures. This case is a three-part juvenile triplane fracture.

12.5 years          13 years          13.5 years          14 years

Figure 5.1
**Pattern of fusion of distal tibia and fibula**

Widening of tibial physeal plate

Vertical fracture of epiphysis

Figure 5.2
**Three-part triplane fracture**

Lucent line traversing tibial metaphysis and epiphysis

Figure 5.3
**Juvenile triplane fracture**

Figure 5.4
**Two-part juvenile triplane fracture**

Figure 5.5
**Three-part juvenile triplane fractures**

# Case 42

Patient fell from climbing frame, injuring ankle.

Describe the radiographs.

What is the name for this type of injury?

# Answer to Case 42

The anterior posterior view demonstrates an oblique fracture through the epiphysis and widening of the physeal plate lateral. This appears to be a Salter Harris type III injury. On reviewing the lateral there is a fracture through the dorsal metaphysis of the tibia, disrupting the physeal plate (the anterior metaphysis and epiphysis of the tibia are no longer in alignment). This appears to be a Salter Harris type II injury. To conclude, this case demonstrates a juvenile triplane fracture (two-part); often a triplane fracture appears as a Salter Harris III on the anterior posterior view, but a Salter Harris II on the lateral view (see Case 41).

Loss of alignment of metaphysis and epiphysis, demonstrating disruption of the physeal plate

Figure 5.6
**Two-part juvenile triplane fracture**

## Case 43

Patient fell, hit medial malleolus on metal bar, now painful.

Describe the radiographs.

Is there a fracture?

## Answer to Case 43

There is a fracture of the medial malleolus. Remember the medial malleolus is made of two parts, called colliculi. The anterior colliculus is long and pointed, the posterior colliculus is short and fat. This is what gives the appearance of a sclerotic line over the medial malleolus, and should not be mistaken as a fracture. In this case there is a step in the cortex and a lucent line distal to the sclerotic line (of the posterior colliculus); hence there is a fracture of the anterior colliculus of the medial malleolus.

Posterior colliculus

Lucent line

Step in cortex

Anterior colliculus

# Case 44

Patient fell down step, inverting ankle, now pain at base of fifth metatarsal.

Describe the radiographs.

Which tendon attaches to the base of the fifth metatarsal?

This tendon lies in close proximity to what other ligament?

# Answer to Case 44

There is a transverse fracture of the base of the fifth metatarsal. The tendon of the peroneus brevis attaches to the base of the fifth metatarsal, and lies in close proximity to the lateral collateral ligament. Inversion of the ankle may stress the lateral collateral ligament resulting in a tear of the ligament or an avulsion fracture of the lateral malleolus, or excessive stress on the peroneus brevis tendon resulting in an avulsion of the base of the fifth metatarsal. Although the clinician when referring for ankle radiography will assess whether there is any bone tenderness to the fifth metatarsal, it is useful in a trauma setting to include the base of the fifth metatarsal on all lateral ankle radiographs to prevent an injury being missed.

With adolescents there is the additional complication of the apophysis at the base of the fifth metatarsal. Apophyses differ from epiphyses in that they do not contribute to longitudinal growth of the bone and are not within a joint. The apophysis at the base of the fifth metatarsal has a vertical orientation, whereas avulsion fractures have a transverse orientation. (Remember the ligament attaches to the inferior border of the base of the fifth metatarsal. Inversion results in a pull inferiorly from the ligaments, resulting in a transverse fracture.)

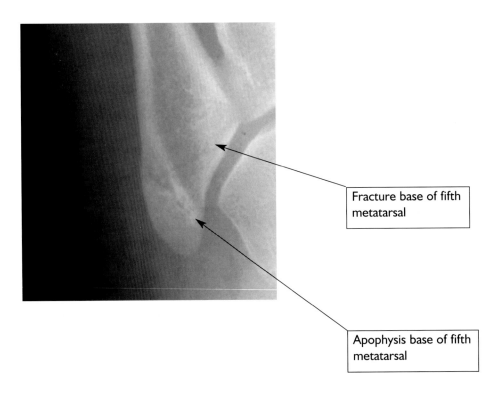

Fracture base of fifth metatarsal

Apophysis base of fifth metatarsal

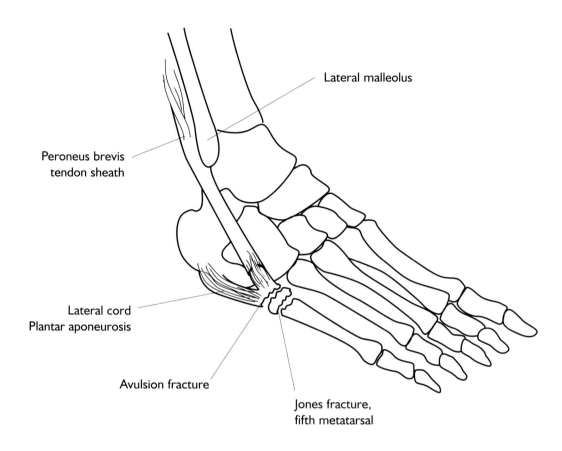

Figure 5.7
**Fractures of the base of the fifth metatarsal**

Figure 5.7 shows fractures of the base of the fifth metatarsal. these are:
● an avulsion fracture of the base of the fifth metatarsal – occurs secondary to an acute inversion injury.
● a fracture at the junction of the metaphysis and diaphysis of the fifth metatarsal – a stress fracture secondary to overuse.
● a Jones fracture – an acute injury of the fifth metatarsal occurring more distally (2–4 cm distal to the base of the fifth metatarsal).

Jones fractures have a high rate of non-union. Therefore it is important to distinguish between avulsion fractures (which are largely treated conservatively) and Jones fractures which require more formal follow-up and aggressive treatment.

# Case 45

Patient fell inverting ankle, soft tissue swelling and pain to fifth metatarsal.

Is there a fracture?

Is there an apophysis?

## Answer to Case 45

There is a transverse avulsion type fracture of the base of the fifth metatarsal. The apophysis of the base of the fifth metatarsal is also visible (vertically orientated – see Case 44).

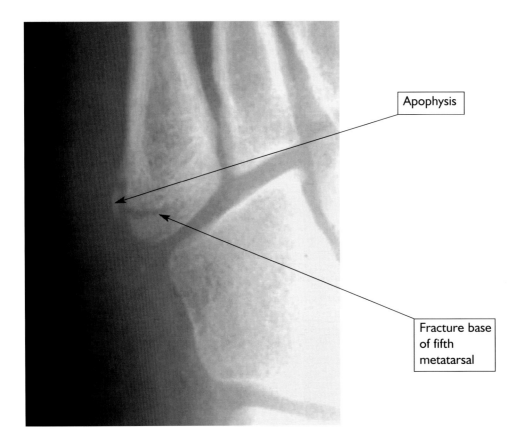

Apophysis

Fracture base of fifth metatarsal

# Case 46

Patient stubbed toes, now painful metatarsal heads.

Describe the radiographs.

Is there a fracture?

Are there any normal variants?

Is trauma a common indication for toe radiographs?

# Answer to Case 46

There is a fracture demonstrated on these radiographs. It is a Salter Harris II of the proximal phalanx of the second toe. There are several normal variants demonstrated on this radiograph. Firstly the second toe does not have a middle phalanx. The proximal phalanx of the second toe appears longer than normal, almost as though the proximal phalanx and middle phalanx had fused together (symphalangia). To have no middle phalanx on the second toe is a common normal variant.

A careful look at the hallux reveals that the proximal phalanx is shorter than normal – it does not have an epiphysis, hence no growth, resulting in a shorter proximal phalanx. Also there is a small triangular middle phalanx on the lateral aspect of the fifth (little) toe.

Radiographs should not be taken to demonstrate fractures of the toes as this does not alter management of the patient (see *Making Best Use of a Department of clinical Radiologists*: Royal College of Radiologists, 2003). However radiographs of the toes may be taken for suspected dislocation, or as in this case when the clinician was querying fracture of the metatarsals (as the results of these radiographs will alter patient management).

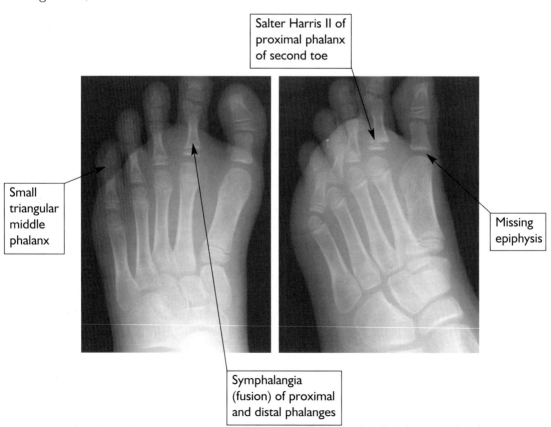

Salter Harris II of proximal phalanx of second toe

Small triangular middle phalanx

Missing epiphysis

Symphalangia (fusion) of proximal and distal phalanges

## Case 47

Patient fell twisting foot, painful metatarsal area.

Name the injury. Name the incidental finding.

Comment on some of the causes of the named incidental finding.

## Answer to Case 47

There is a Salter Harris type II fracture of the proximal phalanx of the third toe. The incidental finding is a dense fragmented navicular. This can be a normal variant of ossification that is a self-limited process, which proceeds to normal ossification. But when associated with pain and when a normal navicular has been demonstrated on previous radiographs then it is likely to be Kohler's disease (avascular necrosis of the navicular). Kohler's disease can be idiopathic, or caused by trauma. It may be a result of stress-related compression of the navicular bone at a critical phase of growth. Often seen in boys aged 4 to 10 years of age, presenting with foot pain and limp.

Salter Harris II of the proximal phalanx, third toe

Dense fragmented navicular

# Case 48

Patient's sibling hit him with a toy car, metatarsal area, now bruising, pain and non-weight bearing.

Describe the radiographs.

## Answer to Case 48

There are buckle fractures of the distal third, medial aspect of third and fourth metatarsals. This coincided with the area of impact and bruising.

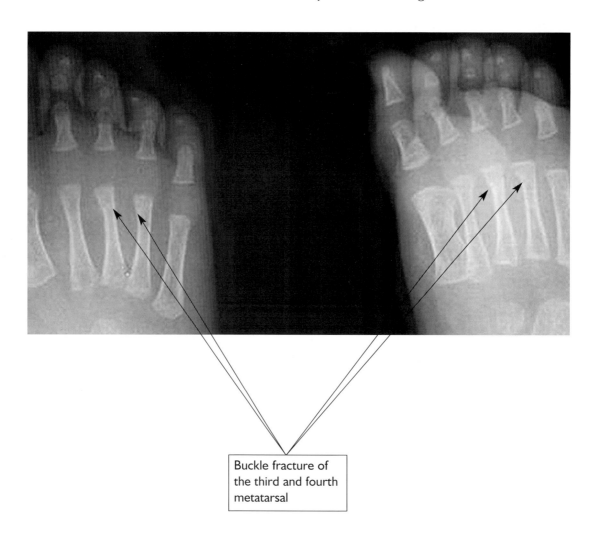

Buckle fracture of the third and fourth metatarsal

# Case 49

Patient stubbed hallux on steps then proceeded to fall down the steps. Pain in hallux, with limited weight bearing.

Is there an injury? If so name it.

# Answer to Case 49

There is an oblique lucent line in the epiphysis of the hallux, with a widening of the physeal plate dorsally. This is a Salter Harris type III injury. Be careful, though, that a bifid epiphysis of the base of the proximal phalanx is not mistaken for a Salter Harris type III injury. With a bifid epiphysis there would be no disruption of the physeal plate as demonstrated in this case.

Widening of physeal plate

Fracture through epiphysis

# Case 50

Patient fell, twisting ankle. Now pain distal fibula and non-weight bearing.

Is there an injury?

## Answer to Case 50

Unfortunately no antero-posterior view is available. An overturned lateral radiograph was taken to better demonstrate the distal fibula, as the pain/injury was associated with this area. A buckle type fracture is demonstrated at the distal fibula.

Buckle of distal fibula

# 6.

# Knee, tibia and fibula trauma

# Case 51

Patient fell from climbing frame injuring knee, now painful, limited weight bearing.

Describe the radiograph?

Is there an injury?

# Answer to Case 51

The lateral view demonstrates a buckle of the proximal tibia; if you look carefully there is a lucent line. The lateral view also demonstrates a faint lucent line traversing the proximal fibula. The anterior posterior view clearly demonstrates the fracture of the proximal tibia – it is a greenstick fracture. The anteroposterior view also demonstrates the lucent line again on the proximal fibula. Hence, as it is demonstrated on both views, it is a definite fracture.

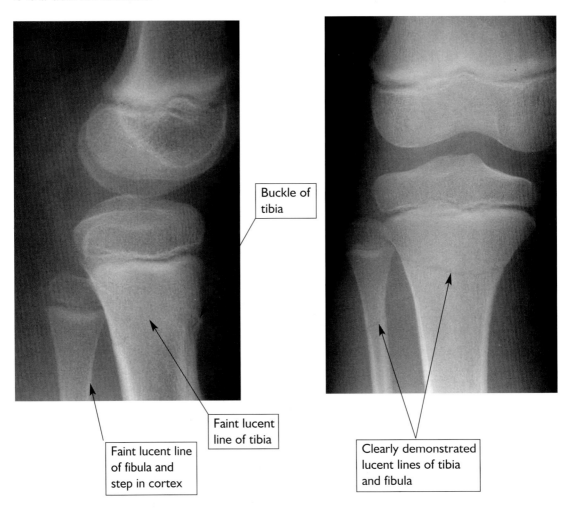

Buckle of tibia

Faint lucent line of tibia

Faint lucent line of fibula and step in cortex

Clearly demonstrated lucent lines of tibia and fibula

Epiphyseal injuries may also occur in the knee, but are relatively rare, Salter Harris II being the most common (70 per cent of physeal injuries of the knee).

The knee, however, is the most common site for a Salter Harris type V injury. They are usually seen in the proximal tibia and are associated with tibial shaft fractures.

# Case 52

Patient presented to accident and emergency after limping for 2 days, no definite history of trauma. On clinical examination there is bony tenderness over tibia.

Describe the radiograph.

Is there an injury? If so, what is the common mechanism of injury?

In what age group does this normally occur?

# Answer to Case 52

There is an undisplaced fracture of the mid-shaft of the tibia. Unfortunately the anterior posterior view is no longer available, but the fracture was not demonstrated on that radiograph. This is commonly called a toddler's fracture; often they are undisplaced and only visible on one radiographic view. Commonly the patient presents to accident and emergency with an acute onset of a limp, without a clear history of trauma. Normally these injuries occur at about 2 years of age; when the child is learning to walk, they fall over, keeping their leg straight, which puts torsion on the calf and resulting in an undisplaced fracture. Recent thinking suggests that for a fracture to be viewed radiographically it must be displaced, so it is perhaps more accurate to describe a fracture such as this as minimally displaced.

In a child of this age, if no fracture is demonstrated on either view, a repeat radiograph in 7 to 10 days reveals a healing response rendering the fracture detectable.

Oblique fracture of mid tibia

# Case 53

Patient fell from bicycle, now painful knee, unable to weight bear.

Describe the radiographs.

Comment on the type of lateral knee view performed in a trauma situation.

# Answer to Case 53

There is an avulsion of the anterior tibial spine at the insertion of the anterior cruciate ligament. This is a common injury in children and adolescents, and occurs at the origin of the anterior cruciate ligament. Over 50 per cent of these injuries are caused by falls from a bicycle, the normal mechanism of injury being hyperextension.

In the trauma situation a horizontal beam knee radiograph should always be taken. This allows assessment of joint effusion (expansion of the suprapatellar bursa to more than 5 mm), and whether a lipohaemoarthrosis is present or not (Figure 6.1). A lipohaemoarthrosis is demonstrated radiographically by a fat fluid level at the supra-patella bursa. A lipohaemoarthrosis is always indicative of fracture, even if no fracture line is demonstrated radiographically, as the only way fat can be in the soft tissue is if it has escaped from the bone marrow following fracture.

Avulsion of anterior tibial spine

Horizontal beam lateral radiograph of normal knee

Normal width of suprapatella bursa – hence no joint effusion

Horizontal beam lateral radiograph demonstrating a joint effusion

Widened suprapatella bursa indicative of a joint effusion

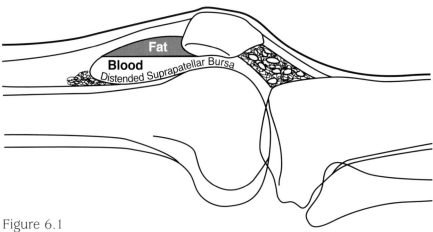

Figure 6.1

**Lipohaemoarthrosis: a horizontal beam lateral radiograph**

Fat fluid line = lipohaemoarthrosis

# Case 54

Patient fell from bicycle, now non-weight bearing, unable to straighten knee.

Describe the radiographs.

Which ligament is involved?

Why is the intercondylar notch seen on the anterior posterior radiograph?

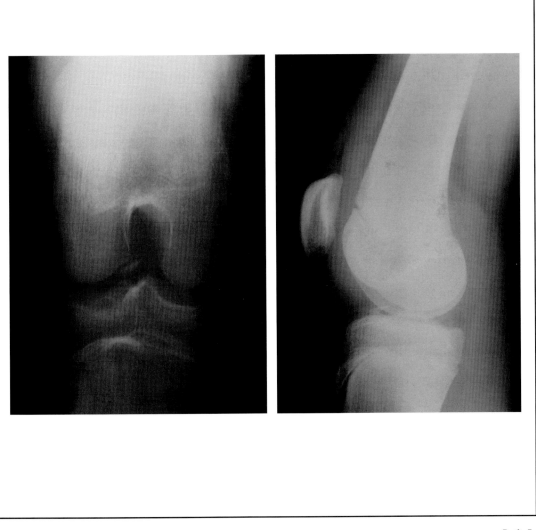

## Answer to Case 54

There is an avulsion of the anterior tibial spine, at the insertion of the anterior cruciate ligament (see Case 53). The horizontal beam lateral radiograph demonstrates that the avulsion is from the anterior tibial spine, and also demonstrates a joint effusion. The intercondylar notch is seen on the anterior posterior radiograph because the patient is unable to straighten their knee, thereby producing the so called 'tunnel view' projection.

Joint effusion

Avulsion from anterior tibial spine

Avulsion

# Case 55

Patient jumped down several steps, now painful knee, particularly over anterior tibial tubercle.

Describe the radiograph.

## Answer to Case 55

There is no bony injury demonstrated on this one radiograph as the tibial tubercle is frequently fragmented, and should not be mistaken for a fracture. However the tibial tubercle can fracture, and frequently follows a 'jumping' injury. It is a common injury in adolescents. The fracture may involve just the tibial tubercle or extend back into the physeal plate. No joint effusion is demonstrated on the horizontal beam lateral radiograph (although one would not be expected with a tibial spine injury).

### Normal tibial apophysis

# Case 56

Patient jumped down from climbing frame, twisting knee.

Describe the radiograph.

## Answer to Case 56

Unfortunately there is no anterior posterior view available. This radiograph demonstrates dislocation of the patella. There is no joint space between the inferior aspect of the patella and superior aspect of the distal femur (the patella appears to lie to one side of the femur instead of in front of it). Patellae normally dislocate laterally, but as there is no anterior posterior view we cannot be sure of this (see Case 58).

## Case 57

Adolescent patient fell, twisting knee, now painful to walk

Describe the radiograph.

## Answer to Case 57

The inferior pole of the patella is raised superiorly; in this area there is a fragment of bone. This is an osteochondral fragment. They commonly occur in adolescents and adults. Mechanism of injury is usually a force directed tangentially to the joint. Common areas for this type of injury are the femoral condyles, talus and capitellum. When just a chondral fragment (i.e. with no bony component) is present, magnetic resonance imaging is required for adequate demonstration.

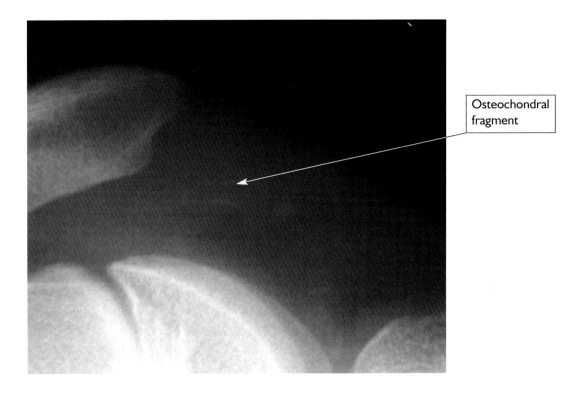

Osteochondral fragment

# Case 58

Patient involved in a road traffic incident. Painful knee, arrived in ambulance with a leg splint on.

Can you see an injury without the benefit of a lateral view?

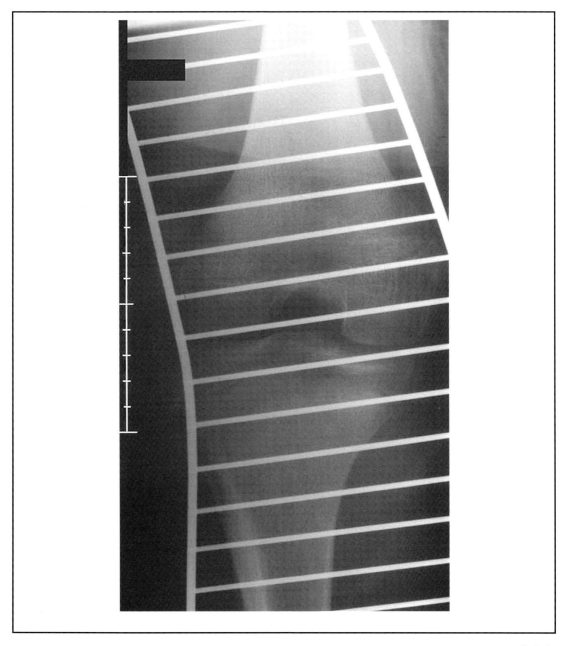

# Answer to Case 58

The splint is very distracting and may hide subtle fractures; consequently it should have been removed prior to x-ray. But a careful look reveals the injury; a lateral dislocation of the patella, which is readily demonstrated on the lateral radiograph.

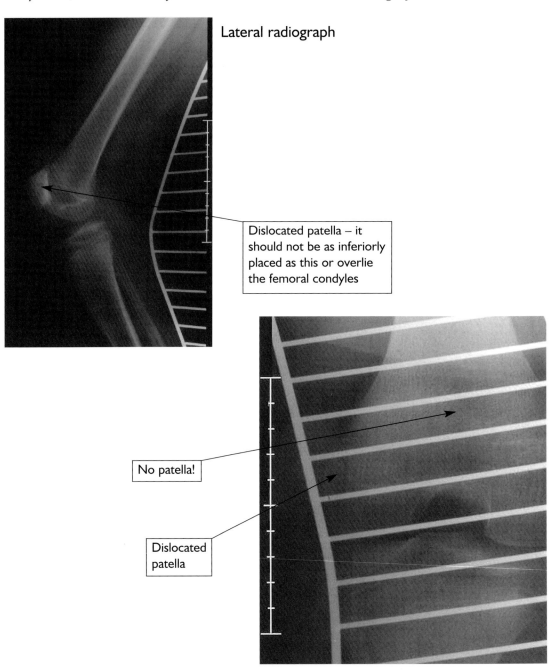

Lateral radiograph

Dislocated patella – it should not be as inferiorly placed as this or overlie the femoral condyles

No patella!

Dislocated patella

Patella dislocation is normally lateral. Patients with patella alta (the patella lies in a higher position relative to the femur than normal), patella tilt and lateral patella displacement are more prone to lateral dislocation or subluxation of the patella. Sometimes the patella as it dislocates can knock off a fragment of bone, which may remain in the joint resulting in reduced movement and locking. Patella alta can be viewed on the lateral knee radiograph (it is elongation of the infrapatella tendon). On the turned lateral view of the knee, with 20 to 30 degrees flexion, the ratio of the infrapatella tendon length (from the inferior pole of the patella to the anterior tubercle) to the length of the patella is 1.0 ±0.2 (Figure 6.2). If this ratio is greater than 1.2, patella alta exists (see Figure 6.3).

A skyline view is required to assess patella tilt and lateral patella displacement, this view is normally taken with the knee flexed by 20 degrees, and as such is not performed in the emergency department, but is normally requested by an orthopaedic surgeon in follow-up clinic.

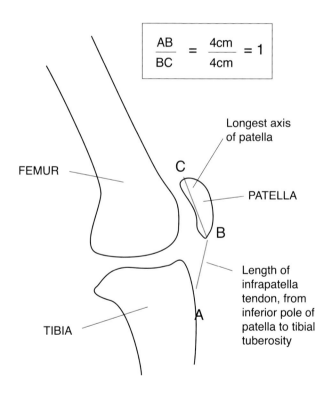

Figure 6.2
**Normal infrapatellar tendon:patella ratio**

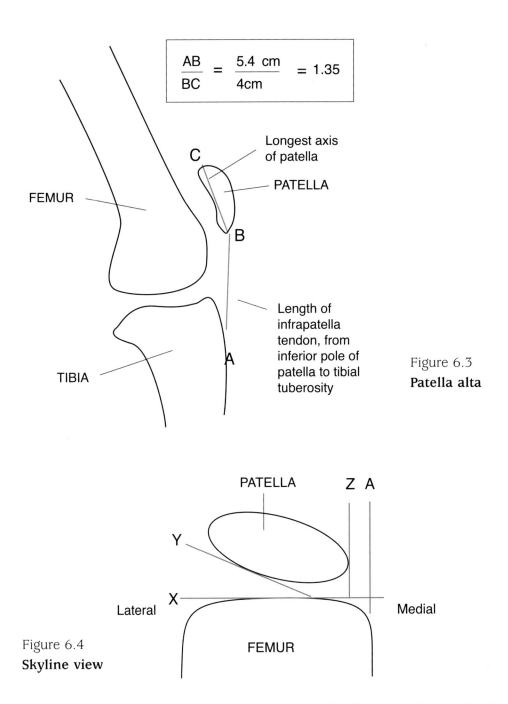

$$\frac{AB}{BC} = \frac{5.4 \text{ cm}}{4\text{cm}} = 1.35$$

C

Longest axis of patella

PATELLA

FEMUR

B

TIBIA

Length of infrapatella tendon, from inferior pole of patella to tibial tuberosity

A

Figure 6.3
**Patella alta**

PATELLA        Z A

Y

X

Lateral

Medial

Figure 6.4
**Skyline view**

FEMUR

X and Y form an angle that normally opens laterally, if it opened medially then there is patella tilt. Line A is perpendicular to line X and at the tip of the medial femoral condyle, line Z is one millimetre lateral to line A and normally intersects the medial patella; if it does not, the patella is laterally displaced and prone to subluxation.

# Case 59

Patient fell off skateboard, then fell again as moving away from other skateboarders. Very painful knee, non-weight-bearing.

Describe the radiograph.

Would another view be helpful?

## Answer to Case 59

There is a torus fracture of the proximal fibula, and an oblique fracture of the fibula more distally. The lateral aspect of the tibial metaphysis demonstrates an irregularity of the cortex, which is probably a fracture. The lateral knee is not a true lateral and was repeated, clearly demonstrating an avulsion type fracture of the posterior aspect of the tibial metaphysis. A careful look at this area reveals the fracture transversing the whole tibia. It is unusual to get two fractures of the fibula, but this case demonstrates the importance of looking very carefully at the whole radiograph even when one fracture has already been identified.

Irregular cortex, probable fracture

Lucent line and change in alignment of fibula

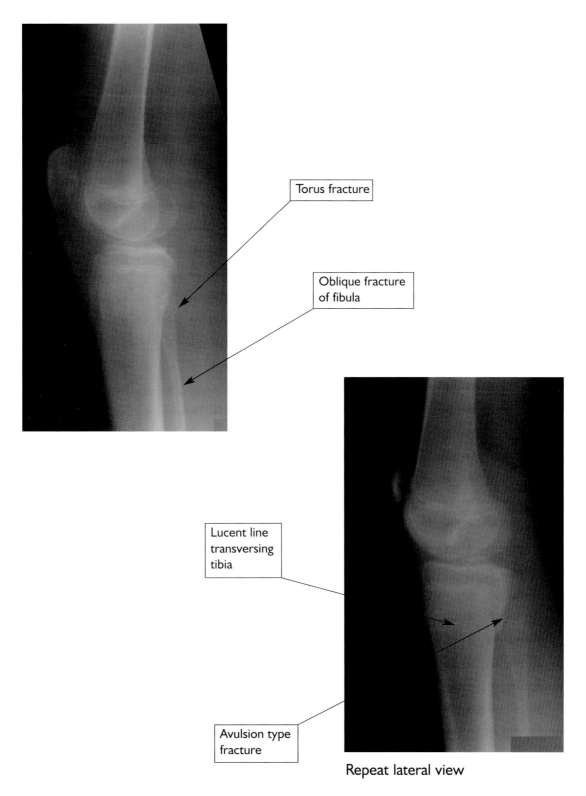

Torus fracture

Oblique fracture
of fibula

Lucent line
transversing
tibia

Avulsion type
fracture

Repeat lateral view

## Case 60

Patient fell whilst skipping, painful tibia and fibula.

Describe the radiographs.

# Answer to Case 60

There is a torus fracture of the proximal tibia (lateral aspect) and a buckle type fracture of the fibula at the same level. This demonstrates the importance of looking carefully at the whole length of both bones on tibia and fibula radiographs, particularly close to both joints (remember the tibia and fibula form a ring-like structure; if you see one injury, look for another). Review the proximal tibia again and it reveals a break in the cortex medial aspect. Hence this is a 'lead pipe' type fracture (see Case 3).

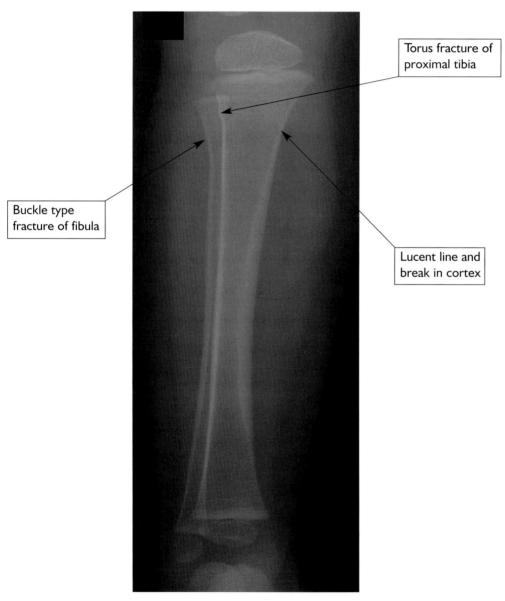

Torus fracture of proximal tibia

Buckle type fracture of fibula

Lucent line and break in cortex

This case demonstrates clearly the difference between a torus fracture and a buckle fracture, although often the terms are used interchangeably to describe the same thing. Buckle fractures appear radiographically as a sharp change in angulation of the cortex, and appear on only one view, while a torus fracture is often demonstrated on more than one view and is rounded in appearance. Think of the moulded profiles of old fashioned skirting boards or the bases of Greek columns – torus fractures look like this (see Figure 6.5). See also case 15.

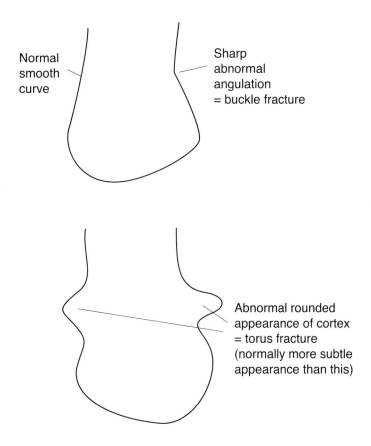

Normal smooth curve

Sharp abnormal angulation = buckle fracture

Abnormal rounded appearance of cortex = torus fracture (normally more subtle appearance than this)

Figure 6.5
**Buckle and torus fractures**

# 7.

# Pelvis and hip trauma

# Case 61

Adolescent patient fell whilst running in games, now painful left hip.

Is there an injury demonstrated on this pelvic radiograph? (View the pelvis before looking at the lateral hip radiograph on the next page.)

In what age group does this injury take place?

Discuss some of the clues found on anterior posterior radiographs to this injury.

# Answer to Case 61

The radiographs demonstrate a slipped femoral epiphysis on the left side. The injury is demonstrated on the pelvis radiograph, and confirmed on the lateral. A lateral radiograph is not always required to confirm this injury – however it is always required to exclude slipped capital femoral epiphysis if this is suspected and it is the patient's first presentation. This is because subtle slips may be missed on the anterior posterior view. Slipped capital femoral epiphysis is a disorder of adolescence – the femoral head appears to slip posteriorly and inferiorly. In fact the femoral head does not move at all; it remains in joint with normal congruity with the acetabulum. What moves is the femoral shaft. Boys are more often affected than girls, particularly overweight, 'Pickwickian' types. This injury tends to occur during the years of rapid growth (10 to 16 years of age), during which the femoral neck changes from valgus to varus; this puts further stress on a growth plate already weakened by rapid growth, hence minor trauma may result in slipped femoral epiphysis. Some studies suggest that an imbalance between growth hormones and sex hormones weakens the physeal plate, rendering it more vulnerable to the shearing forces of weight bearing and injury.

On the anterior posterior radiograph the physeal plate appears wider, with less distinct margins, the epiphysis appears shorter and there is loss of the triangular sign of Capener (a very subtle sign). A line drawn along the lateral femoral neck normally intersects a small amount of the femoral epiphysis (the lateral sixth of the femoral epiphysis) but when the epiphysis has slipped it does not. Remember the pelvis demonstrates both hips so you can compare one side to the other. Disuse osteoporosis of the femoral neck and head may also be demonstrated, on the affected side in chronic cases or acutely on chronic cases (the frog lateral, or horizontal beam lateral radiograph, normally confirms the diagnosis). Figure 7.1 demonstrates the clues to injury on the anterior posterior radiograph, normal being to the left, abnormal to the right.

This case shows the patient with gonad shielding. Normally (in our hospital) at first presentation gonad shielding is not used on anterior posterior or lateral radiographs for females; with males it depends on the area of interest, and is not used in trauma. At second presentation gonad shielding should be used on both sexes on both anterior posterior and lateral views.

**184**

Line along
femoral neck no
longer intersects
epiphysis

Wider indistinct
physeal plate

Normal hip –
line along femoral
neck intersects
epiphysis

Loss of height of
the epiphysis

Loss of alignment of
epiphysis and metaphysis;
epiphysis has slipped
posteriorly and inferiorly
= slipped capital femoral
epiphysis

Lateral view

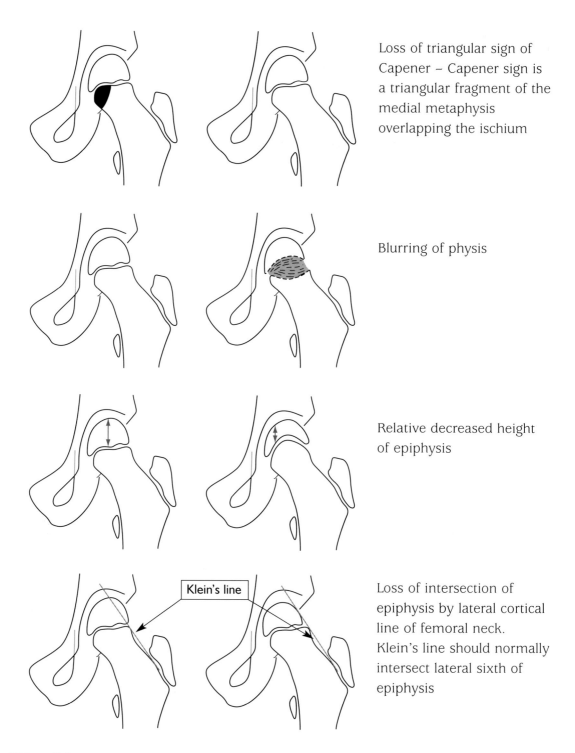

Loss of triangular sign of Capener – Capener sign is a triangular fragment of the medial metaphysis overlapping the ischium

Blurring of physis

Relative decreased height of epiphysis

Klein's line

Loss of intersection of epiphysis by lateral cortical line of femoral neck. Klein's line should normally intersect lateral sixth of epiphysis

Figure 7.1
**Radiographic findings in slipped capital femoral epiphysis (normal on the left)**

# Case 62

Patient was knocked off bicycle, now has pain in hip.

Describe the radiograph.

What are some of the complications of this injury?

## Answer to Case 62

There is a slipped femoral epiphysis of the right hip. If the patient is not treated then exuberant callus will form on the superolateral aspect of the slip forming what is called 'Herndon's hump'. Due to the precarious blood supply to the hip, slipped epiphysis may lead to avascular necrosis (in 25 per cent of patients). Other complications are chondrolysis (in about 30 to 35 per cent of patients), which occurs within one year of slippage and may be evident by gradual narrowing of the joint space. Early arthritic changes are also a complication. Pins are normally inserted following such a slip under image intensifier control.

Anterior posterior view

Frog lateral view

# Case 63

Adolescent fell during school sports day. Now has a painful right hip.

Can you see an injury, before viewing the lateral radiograph overpage?

What is the name of the accessory ossicle sometimes found here?

# Answer to Case 63

There is an avulsion from the anterior iliac spine. If both hips are compared it will be seen that there is no such area on the left hip. However there is a normal accessory ossicle sometimes found here called the os acetabulum. Accessory ossicles are normally well corticated and rounded (difficult to assess this on the pelvis radiograph). The lateral radiograph demonstrates the bony fragment anterior to the acetabulum, confirming it is an avulsion not an accessory ossicle. Notice the normal triradiate cartilage of the acetabulum on these radiographs.

**Lateral view of right hip**

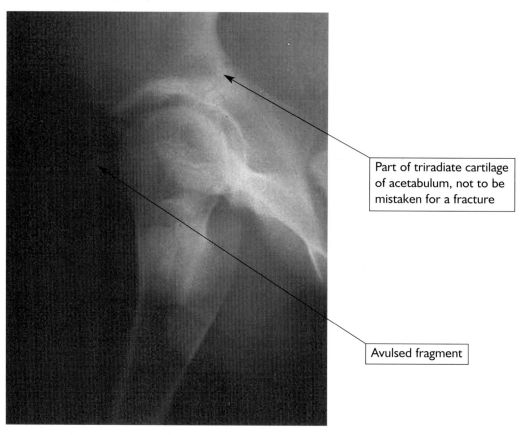

Part of triradiate cartilage of acetabulum, not to be mistaken for a fracture

Avulsed fragment

# Case 64

Cheerleader fell awkwardly, now painful left hip.

Describe the radiographs.

Is there an injury? If so, what ligament is involved?

In what age group do these injuries of the pelvis commonly occur?

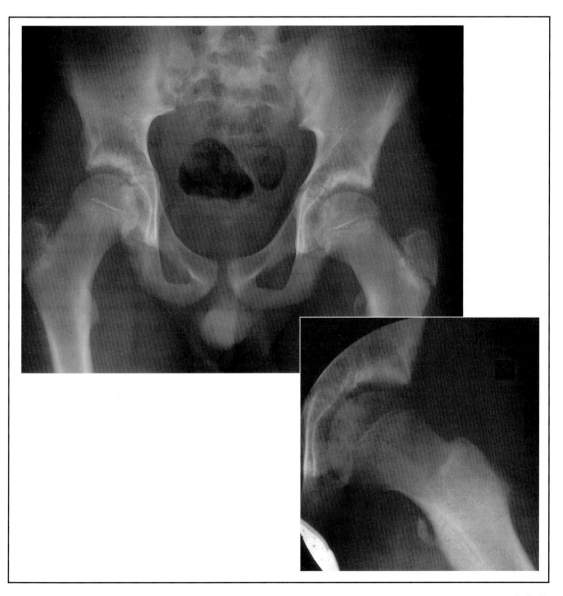

## Answer to Case 64

There is an avulsion of the left lesser trochanter of the left hip (compare one side to the other). Avulsions of the apophyses of the pelvis are common between 12 to 16 years of age. They commonly occur in long-jumpers, sprinters, gymnasts and cheerleaders. The ligament involved in this case is the iliopsoas. Figure 7.2 shows the avulsions of the apophyses that may occur in the pelvis and their attached ligaments. The apophyses are weaker than the ligaments, hence are avulsed during trauma; the same injury occurring in an adult would probably result in tearing of the ligament. Remember the apophyses of the pelvis are the last to fuse at 25 years of age, so potentially avulsions may occur until this age.

One of the most commonly avulsed apophyses is at the ischial tuberosity where the hamstrings attach. When an avulsion occurs here it often lays down lots of bone, which if sufficient can trap the sciatic nerve in later life causing problems sitting down. The gross amount of bone laid down may be mistaken as osteomyelitis or Ewing sarcoma, so care is required – there may not be a history of trauma.

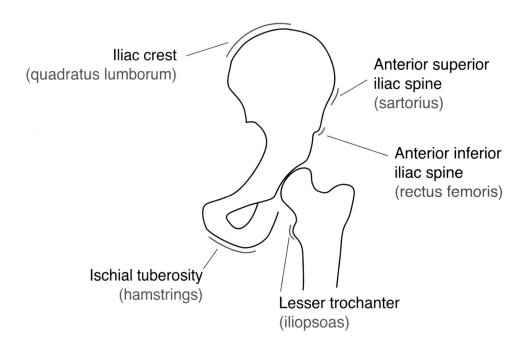

Figure 7.2
**Common sites of apophyseal avulsion and muscle attachment**

# Case 65

Is any injury demonstrated on this radiograph?

Describe Hilgenreiner's line and Perkins' line and their use.

What is the probable cause of the artefacts inferior to the symphysis pubis?

# Answer to Case 65

This is an example of developmental dysplasia of the left hip (DDH), previously known as congenital dislocation of the hip.

It is not related to trauma, but very rarely, as in this case, may be found when presenting to the emergency department regarding some other hip problem. It is painless and may be detected at birth when a baby is checked prior to discharge, or later because of asymmetrical skin creases or leg-length discrepancy or waddling gait (if bilateral).

Hilgenreiner's line is a line drawn from one triradiate cartilage to the other triradiate cartilage; Perkins' line is a line drawn inferior from the anterior inferior iliac spine. The femoral epiphysis should lie in the inner lower quadrant formed by these lines. If the femoral epiphysis is superior to Hilgenreiner's line, it is superior subluxed; if it is lateral to Perkins' line, it is laterally subluxed; if both, it is dislocated. Hence in Figure 7.3 the right hip is laterally subluxed, the left hip is dislocated.

The artefact seen on the pelvis is the baby's nappy. This is very distracting and can hide abnormalities so patients should not have pelvic x-rays with a nappy on.

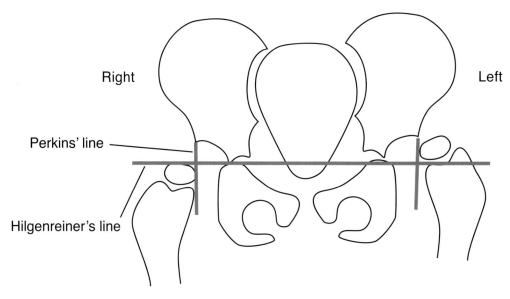

Figure 7.3
**Developmental dysplasia of the hip**

Another case of developmental dysplasia of the hip is shown below.

If you draw Hilgenreiner's and Perkins' line the left hip is dislocated (see anterior posterior image, top). The frog lateral hip (shown above) confirms this, but perhaps was unnecessary as the injury is demonstrated adequately on the pelvis radiograph. The left femoral epiphysis is smaller than the right; this often occurs in developmental dysplasia of the hip and is a secondary phenomenon along with a shallow acetabulum fossa.

## Case 66

Patient with cerebral palsy has less movement than normal in right hip.

Describe the radiograph.

## Answer to Case 66

Patients with cerebral palsy are prone to fractures (whilst being moved by carers, due to disuse osteoporosis); however in this case no fracture can be detected. The right hip has moved laterally and superiorly (remember Hilgenreiner's line and Perkins' line). The right hip has a migration index of 50 per cent; this is likely to be chronic and likely to be painless.

# Case 67

Patient was involved in a road traffic incident.

Describe the radiograph.

# Answer to Case 67

There is a fracture of the left superior pubic ramus and ischial tuberosity. As with adults you should treat the pelvis as a bony ring. If a fracture of the bony ring is identified in one place, look carefully for another. Especially if you see a fracture anteriorly, look at the posterior pelvis and acetabulum area. Remember that Tile and Pennal (1980) divide pelvic fractures into three main mechanisms of injury; lateral compression, anterior compression and vertical shear. The most common mechanism of injury is lateral compression (see p. 202 for a summary of each mechanism of injury). On the left side there is a lucent line in the acetabular roof, and compared to the right hemipelvis the medial acetabulum appears to bulge into the pelvic inlet (there is disruption of the left iliopubic line), indicative of an acetabulum fracture; computerised axial tomography confirmed this. A Judet view was performed, as shown on p. 202, but this is not conclusive concerning the acetabular fracture. Judet views are used to demonstrate acetabular fractures; two oblique views centred on the symptomatic hip, one with 45 degrees medial tilt, one with 45 degrees lateral tilt, are performed.

Remember when assessing children's pelvic radiographs that the sacroiliac joints (S.I. joints) are wider than in an adult, as is the width of the symphysis pubis (2.5 cm in an adult). This is due to the cartilage at these sites, which is not radiographically demonstrated. Also remember not to mistake the triradiate cartilage of the acetabulum for a fracture.

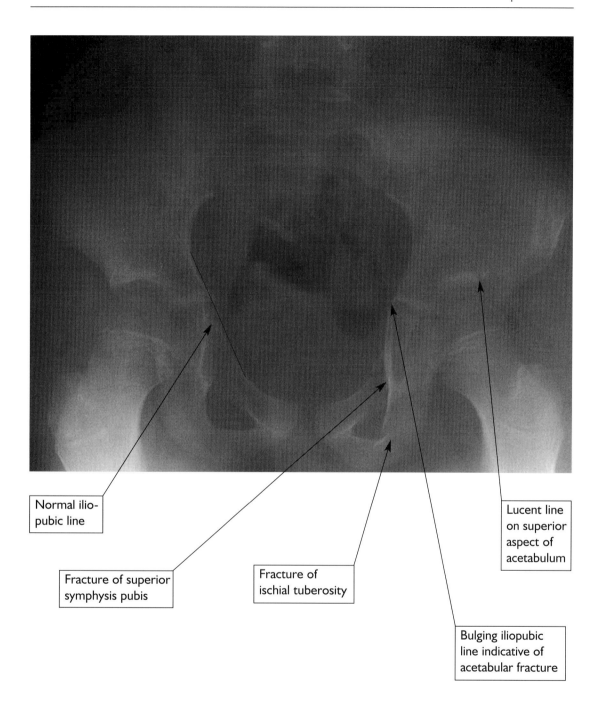

Normal ilio-pubic line

Fracture of superior symphysis pubis

Fracture of ischial tuberosity

Lucent line on superior aspect of acetabulum

Bulging iliopubic line indicative of acetabular fracture

## Judet's view

Triradiate cartilage

Fracture of superior pubic ramus

### Features of *lateral* compression injuries

- Most common bilateral fractures of the superior and inferior pubic rami in the coronal plane.
- Sacral alar fracture impacted.
- Sacroiliac ligaments (both anterior and posterior) remain intact.
- Severe compression may disrupt the posterior ligament complex.

### Features of *anterior* compression injuries

- Results in diastasis of the pubis and sacro-iliac joints.
- Less than 2.5 cm (adults) widening of the symphysis pubis leaves the sacroiliac joints intact.
- More than 2.5 cm (adults) widening of the symphysis pubis is accompanied by disruption of the anterior ligaments of the sacroiliac joints.

### Features of *vertical shear* injuries

- Forces transmitted by the femur to the acetabulum result in vertical displacement of the ipsilateral pelvis.
- Results in fracture of the ipsilateral sacral alar and pubic ramus.
- The posterior sacroiliac ligament complex is disrupted, making the injury unstable.

# Case 68

Patient was involved in a road traffic incident.

Describe the injury.

When reviewing a fracture of the mid shaft of the femur, is there any area you should be concerned about?

# Answer to Case 68

There is a fracture of the left femur proximal third, with foreshortening and lateral angulation of the proximal femur, by about 90 degrees. When there is severe angulation of a fracture of the shaft of the femur concerns should be raised as to whether the hip has dislocated (see Figure 7.4). In this case the epiphysis of the femur does not appear to be in normal alignment with the acetabulum, although the width of the joint space appears normal, hence it is probably not dislocated but requires another view to confirm.

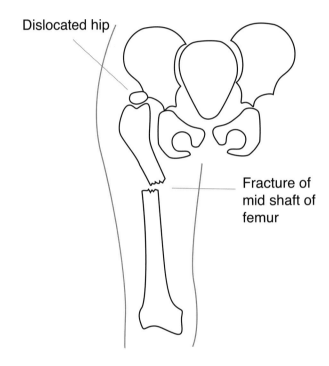

Figure 7.4
**Fracture of midshaft of femur, with associated dislocated hip**

# Case 69

Patient has pain in hip.

Describe the radiograph.

Describe how you evaluate for a joint effusion of a hip on a pelvic radiograph.

## Answer to Case 69

There is a right joint effusion demonstrated by the increased distance between the radiographic teardrop and the metaphysis of the femur compared to the left (see below). Ultrasound is more sensitive for detecting hip effusions.

The right epiphysis is smaller and denser than the left. The right physeal plate is irregular with lucent areas in the metaphysis. The right hip is slightly laterally subluxed (remember to use Perkins' line; see case 65) – this is called Waldenström's sign. This has the radiographic appearance of Legg–Calvé–Perthes disease (often referred to as Perthes disease). It commonly occurs in males between the ages of 3 and twelve years of age, and is bilateral in 10 per cent of cases. The onset may be insidious or sudden. The symptoms are worsened by activity and relieved by rest. It is a self-limiting disease of 2 to 6 years' duration.

The appearances of the right femur are not acute (stage two of Perthes disease); why the patient has exacerbated pain and effusion needs further investigation.

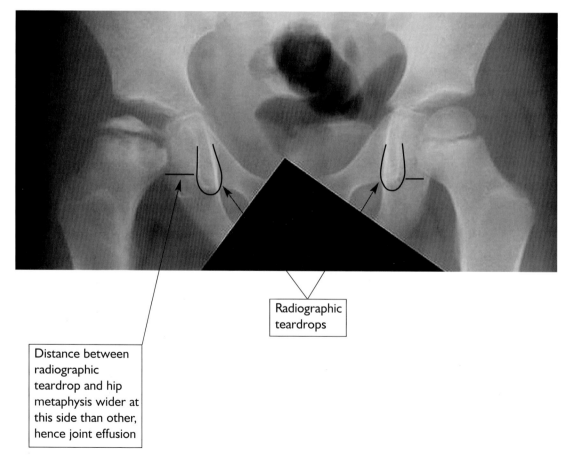

Radiographic teardrops

Distance between radiographic teardrop and hip metaphysis wider at this side than other, hence joint effusion

## Case 70

This young adult has longstanding hip problems.

Describe the radiograph.

What disease process is the most likely cause of this appearance?

Comment on the different stages of this disease and their radiographic appearance.

# Answer to Case 70

There is a flattened left femoral head (mushroom deformity) with a short broad femoral neck (coxa magna). This is the typical appearance of the fourth and end stage of Legg–Calvé–Perthes disease. Below are described the four stages of the disease and their radiographic appearance.

**Stage one** is the avascular stage. The radiographic appearance is joint effusion (widening of teardrop distance) and lateral displacement of the head of femur (Waldenström's sign).

**Stage two** is the necrotic stage. Radiographically the earliest bony appearance is a radiolucent line (crescent sign) in the subchondral bone closest to the articular surface; frog lateral radiographs of the hips are helpful in visualising this. There is increased density of the epiphysis, sometimes referred to as 'snowy cap'; radiolucent areas will develop within the femoral epiphysis (which represent areas of necrotic bone that are undergoing demineralisation). As the disease progresses the epiphysis becomes irregular, fragmented and flattened (collapsed). See Case 69 which is in this phase.

**Stage three** is the healing stage. Dead tissue is replaced by new bone.

**Stage four** is the end stage. Radiographically there is usually a flattened femoral epiphysis (mushroom deformity) and a short broad femoral neck (coxa magna). There may be enlargement of the acetabulum to accommodate the abnormal femoral head – coxa plana – (flattened femoral head), coxa magna (broad femoral head and neck) and coxa valga or vara. Early degenerative changes of the affected hip are common. Coxa valga is an increased neck shaft angle of more than 135 degrees; coxa vara is a reduced neck shaft angle of less than 120 degrees.

# 8.

# Spine, skull and facial trauma

# Case 71

Patient in car seat in a car involved in a collision.

Describe the radiographs.

Comment on the differing radiographic appearances of vascular markings and skull fractures.

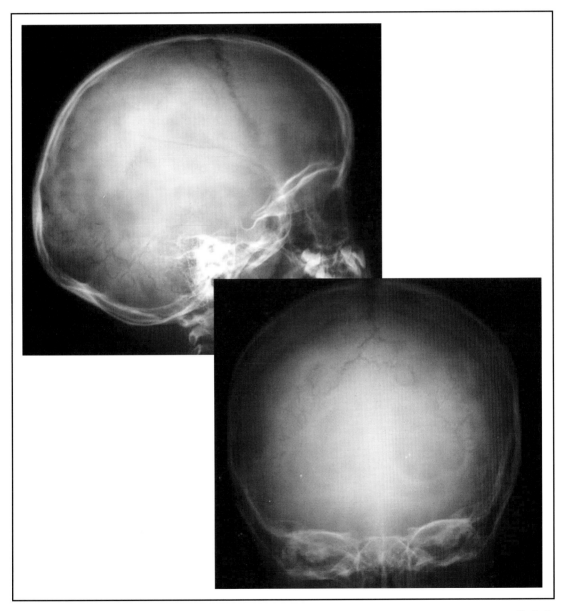

## Answer to Case 71

There is a simple linear fracture of the parietal bone, demonstrated only on the lateral radiograph. The additional importance of identifying this fracture is that the middle meningeal artery lies in this region and may be injured, leading to intracranial bleeding.

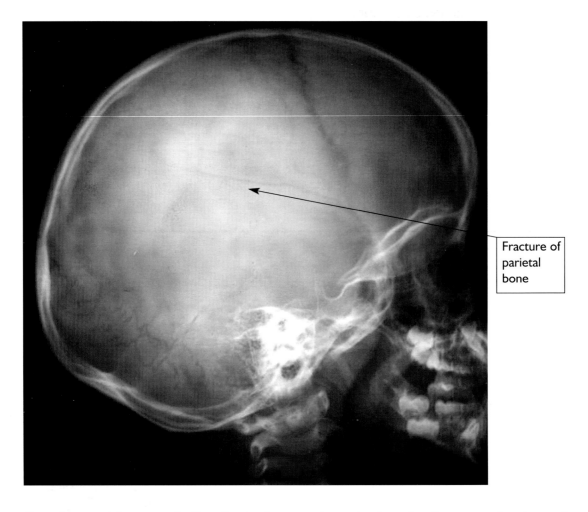

Fracture of parietal bone

Vascular markings on skull radiographs may be mistaken for fractures. In general fractures of the skull appear densely black (this is due to both the inner and outer tables being involved), do not taper or have branches that taper, and do not have sclerotic margins. Vascular markings, however, appear grey on radiographs (as vessels lie in grooves and in the inner table of the skull), have branches that decrease in size, and have sclerotic margins.

Sutures and accessory sutures may be mistaken for fractures. Hence it is imperative to know the position of the normal sutures and the likely position of the accessory sutures, to prevent misdiagnosis (see Case 72 for more on the position of sutures). The concern is not to overlook or incorrectly diagnose a non-accidental injury (see Chapter 1). It is also common to see one or several wormian bones on paediatric skull radiographs. Intra-sutural bone (a wormian bone) is a small area of the skull, normally 1–2 cm in diameter, completely surrounded by a suture.

Wormian bones seen in lamboidal suture

## Case 72

Describe the radiographs.

Comment on the position of the normal sutures. Name the additional sutures that may be found in a paediatric skull.

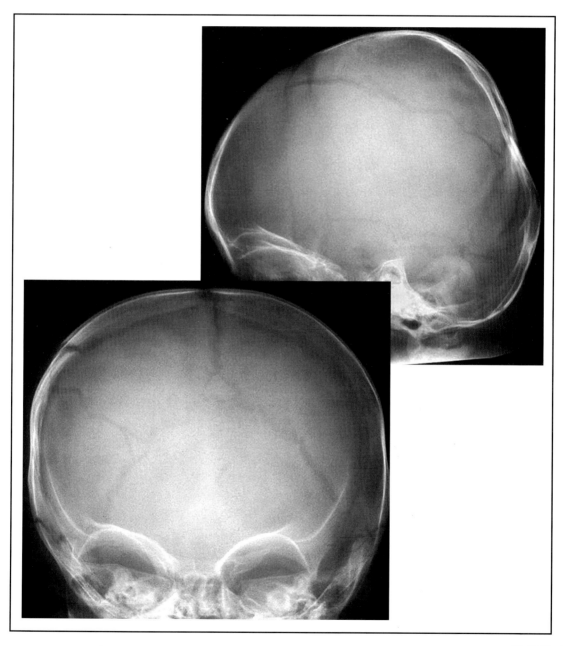

# Answer to Case 72

The initial report read: 'there is a lucent line across the right parietal bone from the coronal suture to the lamboid suture. It takes a wavy course and appears to bifurcate posteriorly. The overall appearances are possibly more in keeping with a unilateral intraparietal suture than a fracture. A similar appearance is seen in Keats' book – see reading list – normal variants that may simulate disease. However, another more senior radiologist's final report read: 'there is a step in the outline of the skull vault on the anterior posterior view and I think this appearance is due to a fracture of the parietal bone rather than a subparietal suture'. This demonstrates what a difficult diagnosis a skull fracture is in a child.

In paediatrics, differentiating a skull fracture from a normal accessory suture can sometimes be very difficult; a sound knowledge of sites of the normal sutures and most common accessory sutures is helpful.

The normal sutures found on skull radiographs are the sagittal, coronal, lamboidal, squamosal, occipitomastoid (Figures 8.1–8.2). Common accessory sutures are the metopic suture (the commonest, which may persist into adulthood, divides frontal bone into two halves), the accessory parietal suture (may be incomplete, vertical, horizontal or oblique), the mendosal suture (extends posteriorly from the lamboidal suture on lateral view, and passes medially on Towne's view) and the innominate suture (always present in infants but disappears as the child matures). See Figures 8.3–8.5.

The NICE guidelines (2003) for assessment and management of head injury advocate that skull films are only needed where there is suspicion of non-accidental injury or where CT is not available, and children need a period of observation. Hence we are seeing fewer skull x-rays and some of the cases in this chapter are old and would today have CT instead.

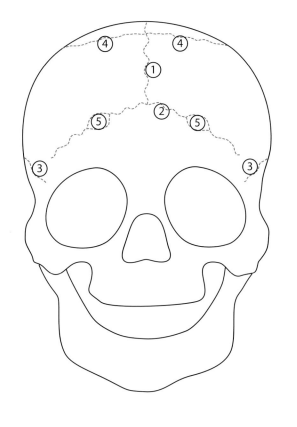

Figure 8.1
**Normal sutures on anterior posterior radiograph**

1 Sagittal suture

2 Lamboidal suture

3 Squamosal suture

4 Coronal suture

5 Wormian bone

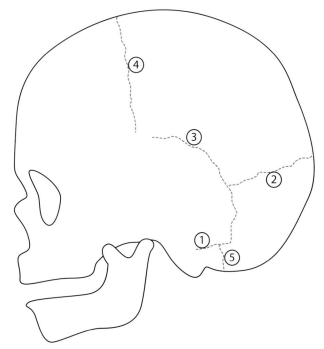

Figure 8.2
**Normal sutures on lateral radiograph**

1 Occipitomastoid suture

2 Lamboidal suture

3 Squamousal suture

4 Coronal suture

5 Innominate suture

Figure 8.3

**Possible positions of accessory sutures on anterior posterior radiograph**

**1** Sagittal suture

**2** Lamboidal suture

**3** Squamosal suture

**4a** Accessory parietal suture

**4b** Accessory parietal suture

**5** Metopic suture

Figure 8.4

**Possible positions of parietal accessory sutures on lateral radiograph**

**1** Occipitomastoid suture

**2** Lamboidal suture

**3** Squamosal suture

**4** Coronal suture

**5** Innominate suture

**A** A complete horizontal accessory parietal suture

**B, C** Incomplete accessory parietal sutures

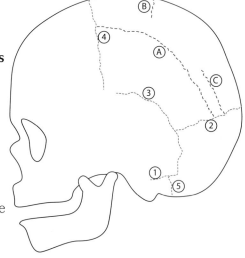

Figure 8.5 **Accessory sutures on a Towne's radiograph**

**1** Sagittal suture

**2** Lamboidal suture

**3** Squamosal suture

**4** Coronal suture

**5** Foramen magnum

**6** Mendosal suture (occasionally it is complete as demonstrated here, but more often it is incomplete)

**218**

## Case 73

Patient was involved in a road traffic accident, now sleepy and disorientated.

Describe the radiographs on this and the following pages.

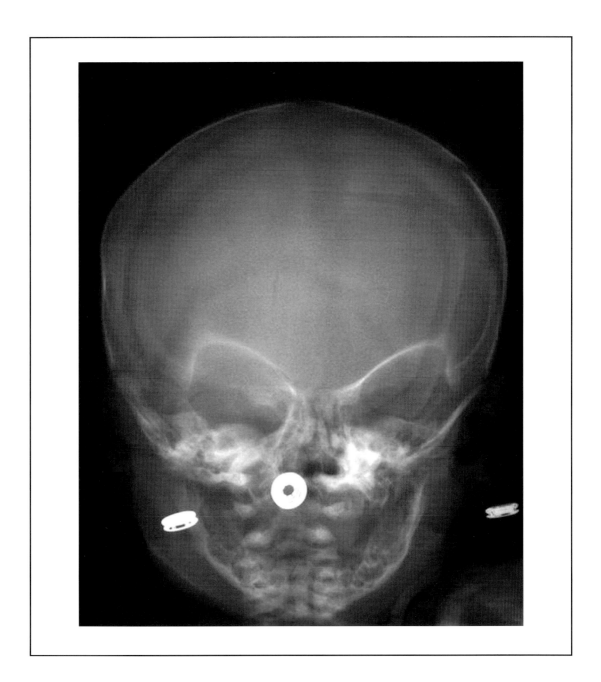

# Answer to Case 73

There is a diastatic fracture of the left parietal bone. This type of fracture requires surgical repair as it is associated with dural tear. Computerised tomography or a magnetic resonance scan may be necessary prior to surgery.

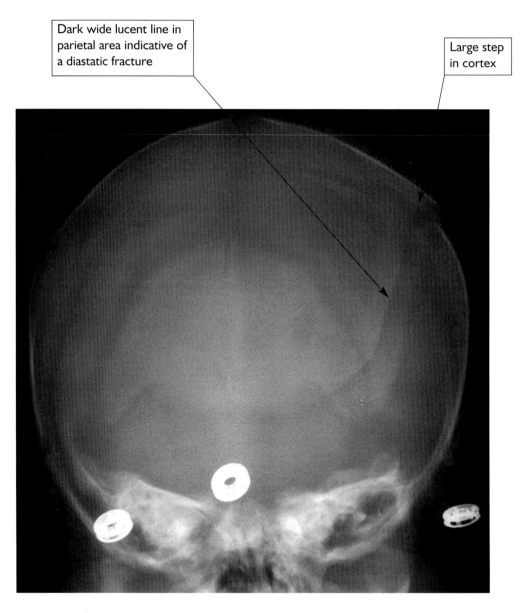

Dark wide lucent line in parietal area indicative of a diastatic fracture

Large step in cortex

# Case 74

Patient was being carried by mother, both fell down a flight of stairs.

Describe the radiographs on this and the following pages.

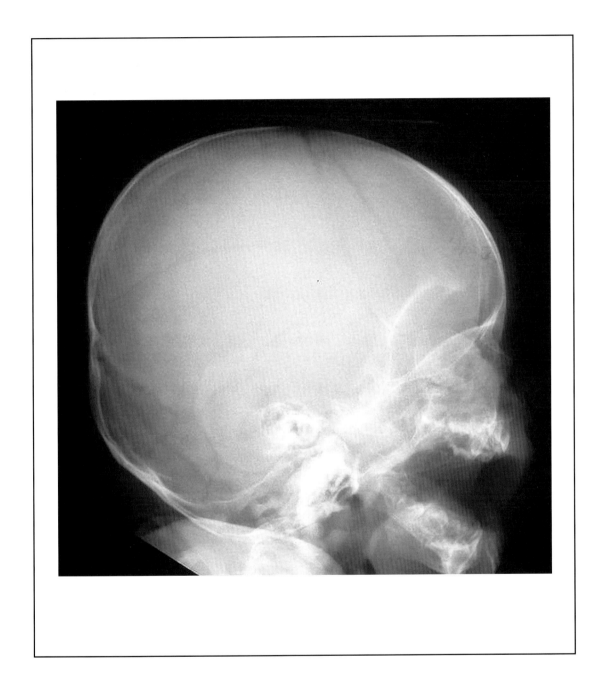

# Answer to Case 74

There is a left parietal skull fracture.

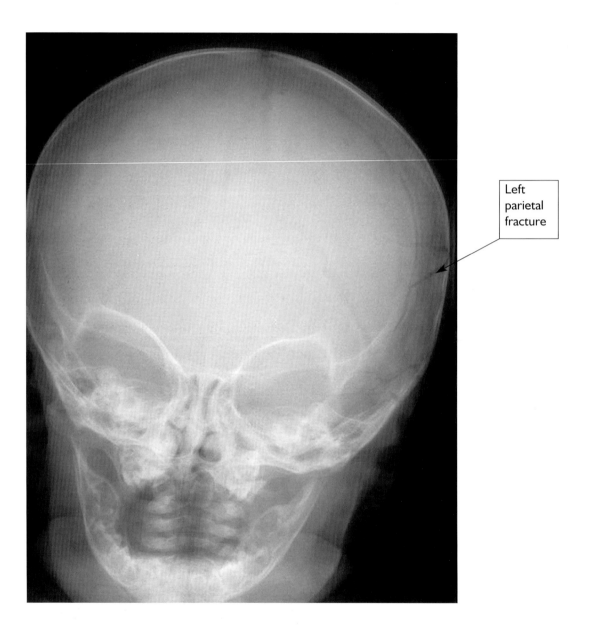

Left
parietal
fracture

# Case 75

Patient was knocked off a bicycle by a car. Drowsy and disorientated with abrasions to the right side of the head.

Describe the radiographs.

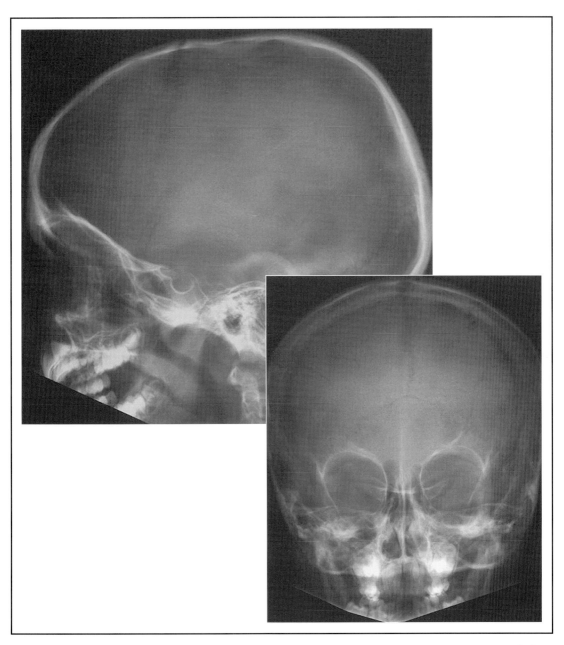

# Answer to Case 75

There is a right parietal fracture.

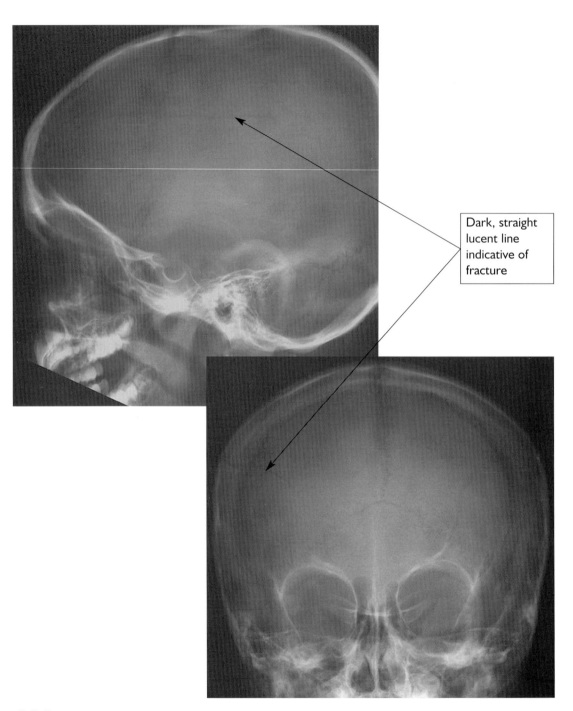

Dark, straight lucent line indicative of fracture

# Case 76

Patient was in a road traffic incident, now pain in neck. Lateral cervical spine x-ray was performed in the resuscitation room.

Discuss the radiograph and findings (if any).

Discuss the pre-vertebral soft tissues in children compared to adults.

## Answer to Case 76

The intervertebral disc space between cervical C7 and dorsal D1 is not adequately demonstrated on this radiograph. This area always needs to be included on a trauma cervical spine whether it be adult or child as this is a common area of injury. There is loss of lordosis which may be due to muscle spasm. There is a slight offset anteriorly at cervical vertebrae C2 and C3. The fulcrum of flexion in adults is cervical vertebrae C5 and C6, whereas in a child it is cervical vertebrae C2/C3. In a young child this may result in a physiological anterior offset of cervical vertebra two on three being visualised on the radiograph; occasionally a similar offset may occur at cervical vertebrae C3/C4. This offset can sometimes be seen up to the age of 30 and should not be mistaken for a fracture. Flexion and extension radiographs were undertaken, which demonstrate the anterior offset even more on the flexion radiograph, but normal alignment is demonstrated on the extension radiograph.

It is debatable whether these flexion and extension radiographs should have been taken, considering the young age of the patient, and that the original radiograph is normal, i.e. no evidence of trauma. We must often balance the risk of missing a spinal injury against exposure to extra radiation. Perhaps in this case there were neurological signs that warranted extra views.

The pre-vertebral soft tissues in adults should not be greater than 5 mm at cervical level C3 and C4, and less than 22 mm at cervical vertebra C6; greater distances than this are indicative of effusion and cervical injury. In children the distances are different; the pre-vertebral soft tissue should be two-thirds the width of the body of C2 at the C3/4 level and not more than 14 mm at C6.

Inherent elasticity in the paediatric cervical spine can allow severe spinal cord injury to occur in the absence of x-ray findings. This is called SCIWORA syndrome – Spinal Cord Syndrome WithOut Radiological Abnormality. In this case magnetic resonance imaging (MRI) is helpful.

The features of SCIWORA were first defined in 1982 by Pang and Wilerger as 'objective signs of myelopathy as a result of trauma with no evidence of fracture or ligamentous instability on plain spine radiographs'. Delayed onset of SCIWORA in children as late as 4 days post injury has been documented.

## Case 77

Patient was involved in a road traffic accident. Radiographs were taken in the resuscitation room.

Is there a fracture present?

# Answer to Case 77

There is no fracture present. On the anteroinferior border of cervical vertebra bodies C3 to C6 can be seen the ring apophyses of the vertebral bodies, not to be mistaken for fractures. Again there is slight offset at cervical vertebrae C3/C4 (as discussed in Case 76) and loss of lordosis. The anterior posterior and peg views taken later demonstrated no injury. As the patient later revealed no clinical signs of neck injury, the clinicians concluded there was no cervical spine injury.

Ring apophysis

C/Spine LAT
CERVICAL SPINE

# Case 78

This 15-year-old was involved in a fight, receiving a blow to the left side of the face.

Is there an injury?

## Answer to Case 78

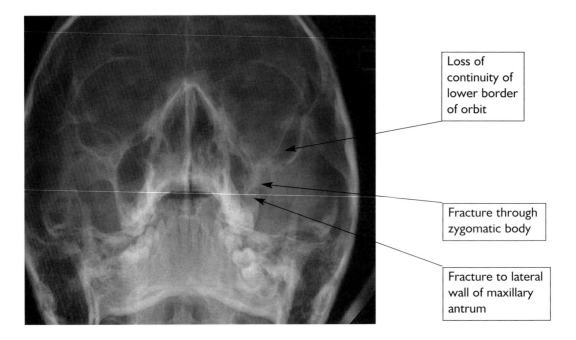

Loss of continuity of lower border of orbit

Fracture through zygomatic body

Fracture to lateral wall of maxillary antrum

In the older adolescent, facial injuries are similar to those in adults. As with adults, look for fluid levels or loss of air in the maxillary antra, as a clue to injury of the facial bones.

A common fracture of the facial bones in an adult is a tripod fracture, involving widening of the zygomaticofrontal suture, fracture of the zygomatic arch, and a fracture through the zygomatic body. This case has three fractures, but only one of the above-mentioned tripod fractures – the fracture of the zygomatic body. When one fracture is visualised, remember to assess the radiographs for other fractures. Dolan's lines are useful when assessing facial trauma, to ensure an orderly search for injury (more cases and information on adults facial and spinal injuries appear in another book in this series).

# Case 79

A younger child was hit in the face, resulting in pain and bruising.

Is there an injury?

# Answer to Case 79

No bony injury was demonstrated. Notice the adult teeth appearing to be in the maxillary antra.

# 9.

# A selection of cases

## Case 80

Patient thought to have fallen. Is now non-weight bearing with pain on touching leg.

Describe the radiographs.

# Answer to Case 80

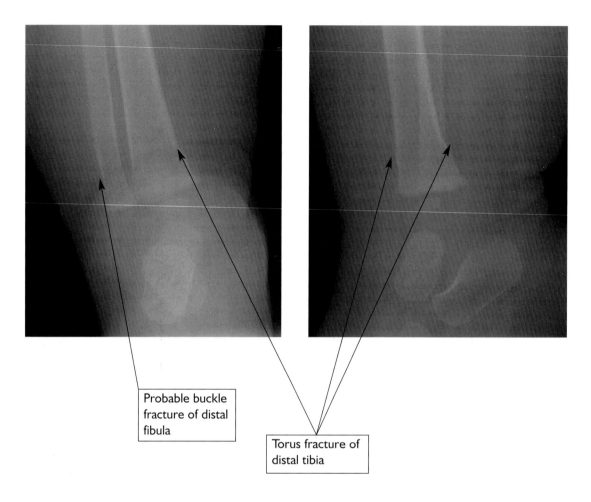

Probable buckle fracture of distal fibula

Torus fracture of distal tibia

There is a torus fracture of the distal tibia and a probable buckle fracture of the distal fibula. This highlights the importance of looking carefully at the whole radiograph especially at both bones on tibial and fibular and radial and ulnar radiographs.

# Case 81

Patient fell down several steps whilst playing, now unable to weight bear, and pain in ankle.

Describe the radiographs.

Would another view be helpful?

# Answer to Case 81

The anterior posterior radiograph demonstrates a sharp lateral angulation of the fibula, typical of a buckle type fracture (see Case 60), but on closer observation a break in the lateral cortex is demonstrated, therefore this is a greenstick fracture. If one fracture is demonstrated check for a second fracture (as mentioned in case 60); there is a break in the cortex of the lateral aspect of the tibia proximal to the fibular fracture – a greenstick fracture. This area is not fully shown on the ankle views and requires full length tibia and fibula radiographs to demonstrate the full extent of the tibial fracture.

Fracture of fibula

Greenstick fracture of tibia

Greenstick fracture of distal fibula with angulation

# Case 82

Patient stubbed toes, now painful toes and metatarsals.

Describe the radiographs.

# Answer to Case 82

There is a Salter Harris type II fracture of the proximal phalanx of the fourth toe.

Salter Harris II of proximal phalanx of the fourth toe

# Case 83

Patient fell onto outstretched hand, now not using elbow.

Describe the radiographs.

# Answer to Case 83

There are raised anterior and posterior fat pads (a joint effusion). The anterior humeral line, instead of passing through the anterior part of the middle third of the capitellum, passes anterior to the capitellum. Both these points are indicative of a supracondylar fracture. There is a fracture demonstrated on the medial and volar aspect of the distal humerus (see Cases 16 and 17).

## Case 84

Patient fell, now with pain in clavicle.

Is there an injury?

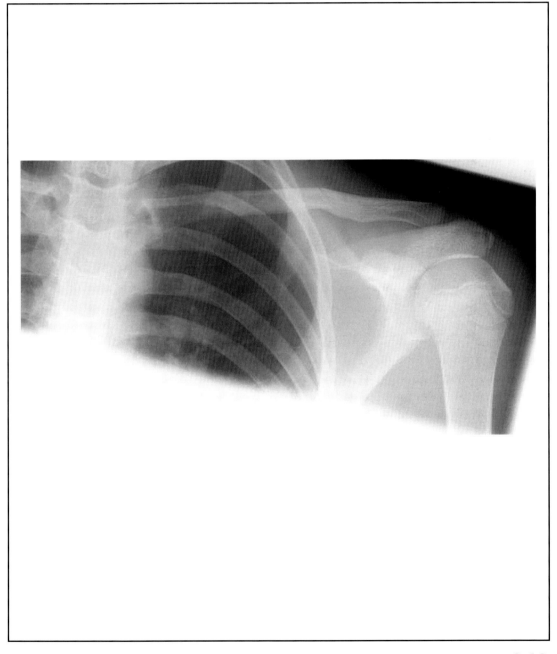

## Answer to Case 84

There is a fracture mid shaft of the clavicle. Sometimes this can be a difficult area to visualise radiographically, requiring a cranially angulated radiograph. (See Cases 26 and 28.)

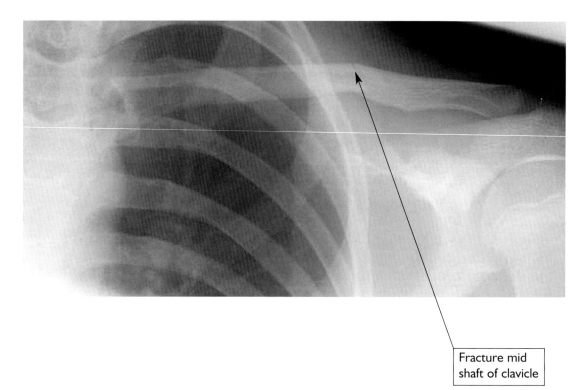

Fracture mid
shaft of clavicle

# Case 85

Patient fell, inverting ankle, now painful weight-bearing.

Describe the radiographs.

# Answer to Case 85

There is a transverse type fracture of the distal fibula (Weber A), with soft tissue swelling. Danis and Weber classified ankle injuries according to the level of the fracture of the fibula. Weber A is a fracture below the ankle joint, Weber B at the joint level (with 50 per cent chance of instability due to involvement of the tibiofibular syndesmosis), and Weber C is a high fibular fracture with instability.

# Case 86

Patient fell onto shoulder, tender head of humerus and acromio-clavicular joint.

Review the shoulder radiographs first, then assess the acromio-clavicular joint radiographs on the next page.

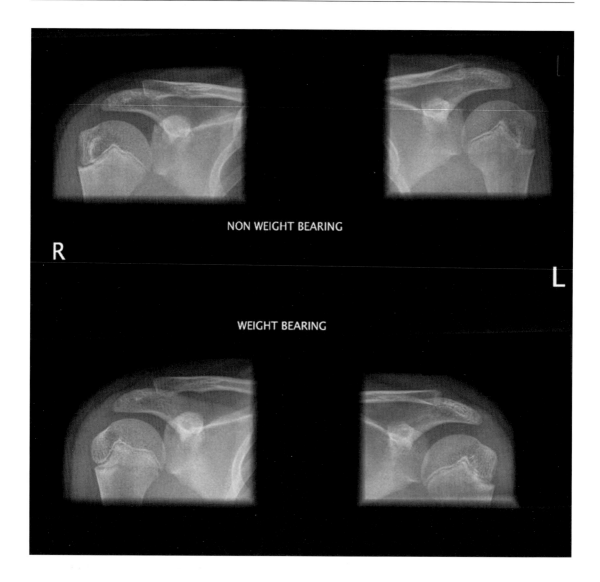

NON WEIGHT BEARING

R

L

WEIGHT BEARING

# Answer to Case 86

The shoulder radiographs show no bony injury; however the anterior posterior radiograph is of poor quality, and the arm is internally rotated instead of externally rotated, possibly masking some pathology.

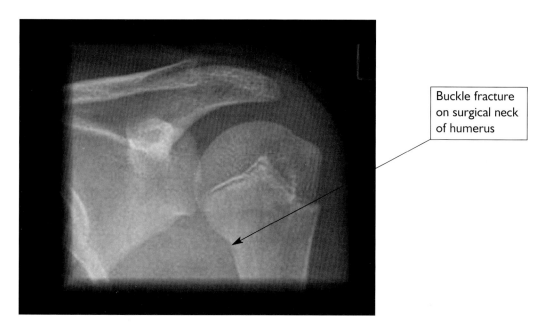

Buckle fracture on surgical neck of humerus

On reviewing the acromioclavicular joint views, the acromio-clavicular joints are aligned normally (remember to check the alignment of the undersurface of the acromion and clavicle when looking for subluxation). On the second group of radiographs the left arm is in the true anteroposterior position with the arm externally rotated, and demonstrates a buckle fracture of the medial aspect of the surgical neck. This emphasises the importance of obtaining as high a quality radiograph as possible, in order not to miss an injury.

# Case 87

Patient fell directly onto elbow, now painful olecranon.

Describe the radiographs.

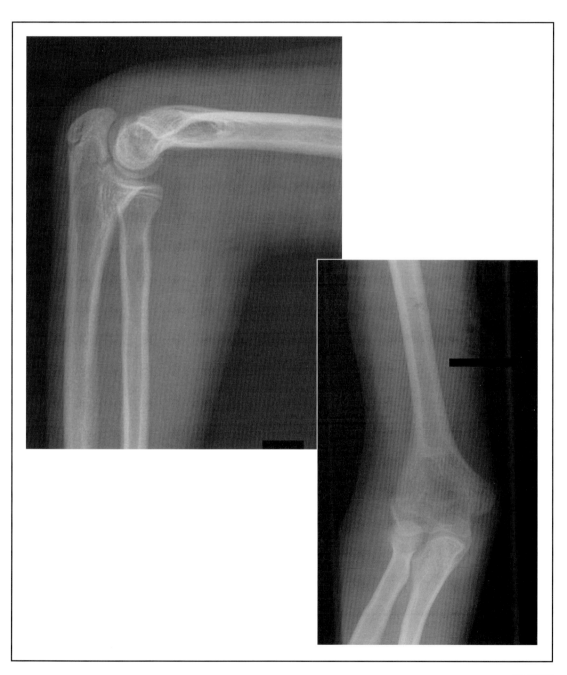

# Answer to Case 87

There is a joint effusion (positive anterior and posterior fat pads) with a fracture of the olecranon process involving the olecranon notch. This is not to be confused with the normal olecranon apophysis (see Cases 16 and 17).

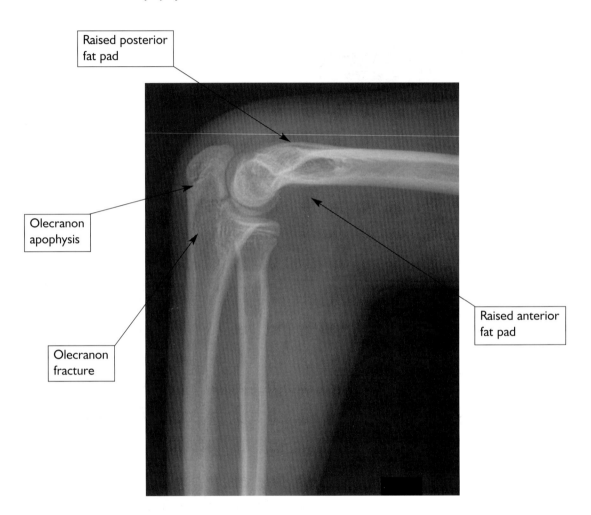

Raised posterior fat pad

Olecranon apophysis

Olecranon fracture

Raised anterior fat pad

# Case 88

Patient fell from wall injuring their ankle.

Describe the radiographs.

# Answer to Case 88

There is a Salter Harris type II injury of the distal tibia. The lateral view demonstrates the malalignment of the anterior tibia metaphysis and anterior tibia epiphysis, clearly demonstrating that the physeal plate is involved in the injury.

Fracture line is in tibia, as it stops at tibial physeal plate. Fibula physeal plate is more distal.

Malalignment of tibia epiphysis and metaphysis demonstrating disruption of the physeal plate

# Case 89

Patient fell from trampoline, now painful ankle.

Describe the radiographs.

Would any other radiographic views be helpful?

## Answer to Case 89

There is a large joint effusion (see short arrows below). There is a fracture of the distal tibia metaphysis which appears to stop at the tibial physeal plate. There is malalignment of the tibial metaphysis and epiphysis indicating disruption of the physeal plate (within the circled area). This appears to be a Salter Harris II of the distal tibia as in Case 88, although a little more subtle. On closer inspection there appears to be widening of the tibial physeal plate laterally and a hint of a lucent line through the epiphysis. An oblique view is required to rule out a triplane fracture.

Effusion

Fracture

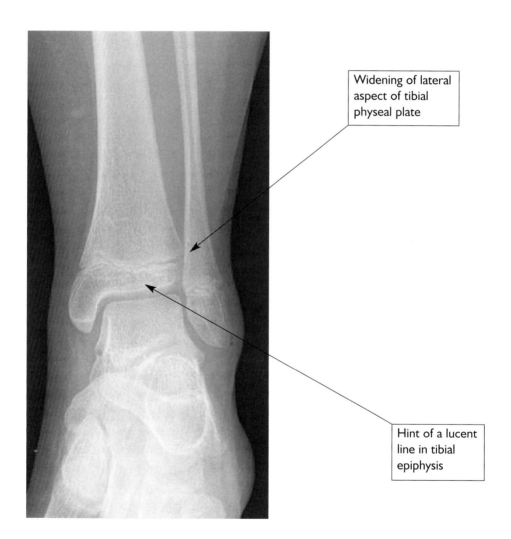

Widening of lateral aspect of tibial physeal plate

Hint of a lucent line in tibial epiphysis

The oblique view below clearly demonstrates a fracture through the epiphysis. This is a two-part triplane fracture (Figure 9.1) which requires different management to a Salter Harris II fracture of the distal tibia. See Case 41.

Fracture
through
epiphysis

figure 9.1
**Two-part juvenile triplane fracture**

# Case 90

Patient fell from bicycle, injuring knee.

Describe the radiographs.

## Answer to Case 90

There is a subtle buckle fracture of the medial aspect of the proximal tibial metaphysis. The indentation on the superior aspect of the proximal tibia is normal and is the area where the tibial tuberosity will form.

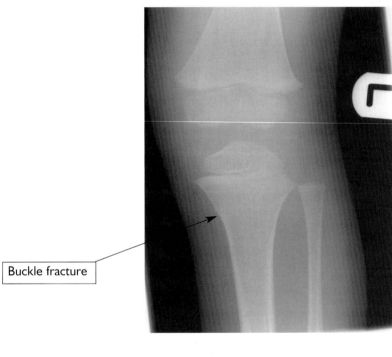

Buckle fracture

Normal tibial indentation, where tibial tuberosity will form

# Case 91

Patient fell on outstretched hand. Now has a painful forearm, unable to move.

Describe radiographs.

# Answer to Case 91

The forearm radiograph demonstrates a torus fracture of the dorsal aspect of the distal radius, with slight dorsal angulation of the distal part (remember the distal radius is normally angulated 10 to 15 degrees volarly). If you the review the elbow on the same radiograph there is a break in the cortex of the distal humerus lateral aspect. Following this, a lateral elbow radiograph was taken; this not only demonstrates a joint effusion (positive anterior and posterior fat pads) and supracondylar fracture, but also a fracture of the proximal olecranon.

# Case 92

Patient hyper-extended fingers during games. Now has a painful little finger metacarpal.

Describe the radiographs.

# Answer to Case 92

There is a Salter Harris type II fracture of the proximal phalanx of the little finger, ulnar aspect.

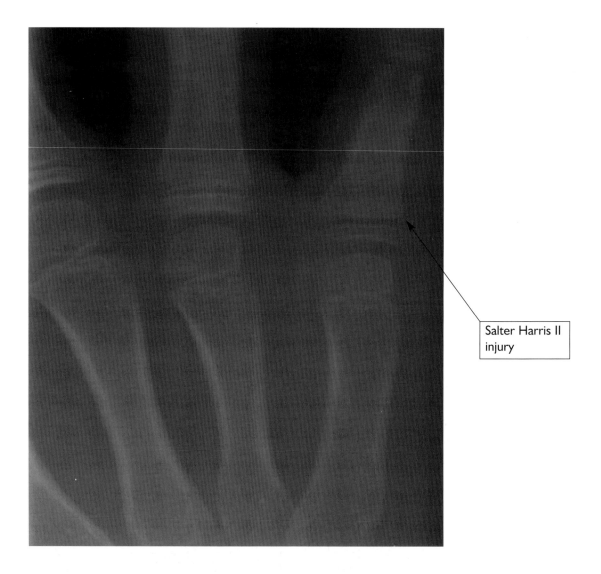

Salter Harris II injury

# Case 93

Adolescent fell during football training, injuring ankle.

Describe the radiographs.

## Answer to Case 93

There is a juvenile Tillaux fracture. A careful look at the peroneal groove demonstrates a step in the cortex and a lucent line in the distal lateral tibia. The fracture is also demonstrated on the lateral view anterior to the distal fibula (see Case 41).

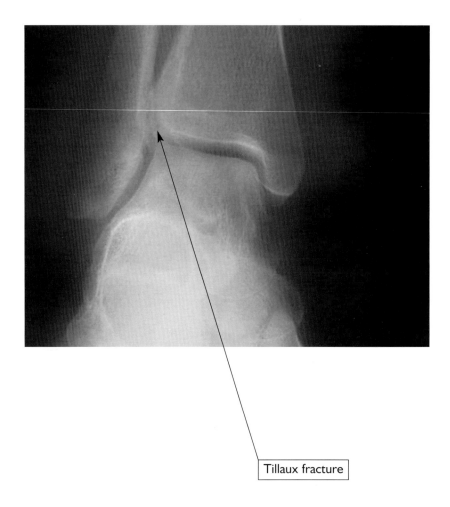

Tillaux fracture

# Case 94

Patient plays cricket frequently, is suffering from pain and stiffness in elbow and has restricted movement.

Describe the radiographs.

What is the name for this condition?

## Answer to Case 94

There is a joint effusion (positive posterior and anterior fat pads). The cortex of the capitellum is irregular, with subarticular lucency and small sclerotic area. This is Panner's disease, avascular necrosis of the capitellum, sometimes called 'little leaguer's elbow', because of its frequency in young baseball players. Normally occurs in males between 5 and 10 years of age. Clinically the patient has pain and stiffness, with restricted range of movement. The radiograph may demonstrate joint effusion, sclerosis, fragmentation and decreased size of the capitellum.

Another case of Panner's disease with more fragmentation of the capitellum is demonstrated below.

# Case 95

Patient fell from tree, now painful forearm.

Describe the radiographs.

## Answer to Case 95

There is a subtle torus fracture of the distal radius, with some increase in volar angulation of the distal radius.

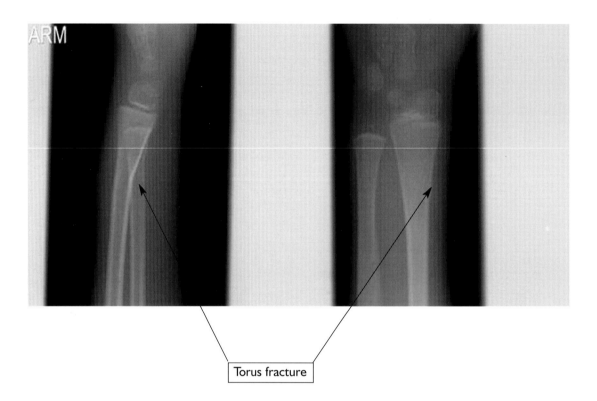

Torus fracture

# Case 96

Adolescent fell onto outstretched hand, now bony tenderness in scaphoid.

Describe the radiographs.

What is the main complication with scaphoid injuries?

# Answer to Case 96

There is a transverse fracture of the distal radius (at the level of the closing physeal plate), with a second longitudinal fracture line. The lateral radiograph shows dorsal angulation of the distal radius. Although the Stetcher's view is too underpenetrated to be diagnostic, the other radiographic views do not demonstrate a scaphoid fracture. Scaphoid fractures and carpal injuries are rare under 12 years of age (see Case 1).

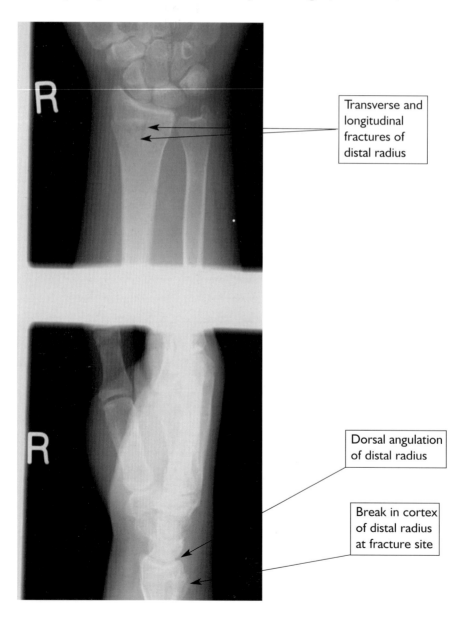

Transverse and longitudinal fractures of distal radius

Dorsal angulation of distal radius

Break in cortex of distal radius at fracture site

The scaphoid has two blood supplies, one at the distal pole, the other at the waist of the scaphoid; the supply at the waist is a development or continuation of a division of the radial artery that also supplies the distal pole. Most fractures occur at the waist of the scaphoid. A fracture at the waist of the scaphoid may affect the blood supply at the waist resulting in avascular necrosis of the proximal pole of the scaphoid. A fracture of the distal pole of the scaphoid will not result in avascular necrosis – as the distal fragment will receive its blood supply from the distal blood vessels, whilst those entering at the waist will supply the rest of the scaphoid. Fractures of the proximal pole of the scaphoid will result in avascular necrosis of the proximal fracture as it is cut off from its blood supply at the waist and distally. Scaphoid fractures are at risk from delayed union, non-union and avascular necrosis of the proximal pole.

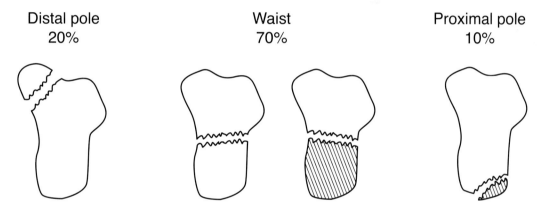

Figure 9.2
**Scaphoid fractures – shaded areas highlight areas at risk from avascular necrosis following fracture**

**279**

Below is another patient with non-union of the scaphoid and avascular necrosis following fracture.

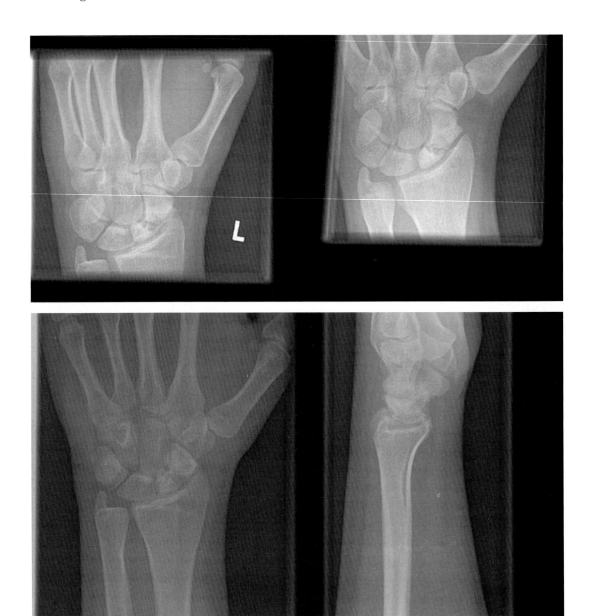

# Case 97

Patient hit a wall.

Describe the radiographs.

## Answer to Case 97

There is a greenstick fracture (notice break in cortex volar aspect) of the distal part of the fifth metacarpal (little finger metacarpal), with some volar angulation of the distal part. It is a typical injury following a direct blow with the clenched fist.

Break in cortex volar aspect of metacarpal, hence greenstick type fracture.

# Case 98

Patient fell from bike, injuring knee.

Describe the radiographs.

## Answer to Case 98

There is no bony injury. The bifid patella is a normal development variant and not a fracture, which will continue to form a bipartite patella.

# Case 99

Patient fell onto outstretched hand, now bony tenderness of distal radius.

Describe the radiographs.

# Answer to Case 99

There is a subtle buckle fracture of the distal radius, ulnar aspect, which coincides with the site of bony tenderness.

Buckle in cortex
indicative of a
fracture

# Case 100

Patient fell, inverting foot.

Describe the radiographs.

# Answer to Case 100

There is a transverse fracture of the base of the fifth metatarsal (see Cases 44 and 45) with associated soft tissue swelling.

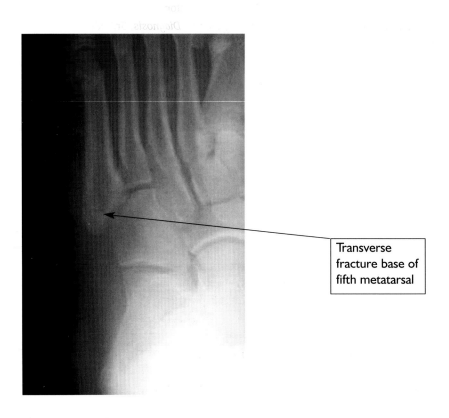

Transverse fracture base of fifth metatarsal

# Reading List /Bibliography

Annals of the ICRP (1996). *Use of Ionising Radiation and its Application in Diagnostic Imaging:* London:ICRP.

Borden, S. (1975). 'Roentgen recognition of acute plastic bowing fractures of the forearm in children' in *American Journal of Radiology* 124, 524.

Burnett, S., and Tyler, A. (2000). *A–Z of Orthopaedic Radiology*. London: W.B. Saunders. ≈

Caffey, J. (1978). *Paediatric X-ray Diagnosis,* 7th edn. London: Year Book Medical Publishers.

Carty, H. (2004). *Imaging Children*, 2nd edn. London: Churchill Livingstone.

Chapman, S. and Nakielny, R. (1995). *Aids to Radiological Differential Diagnosis*, 3rd edn. London: W.B. Saunders.

Crowe, J.E. and Swischuk, L.E. (1977). 'Acute bowing fractures of the forearm in children: A frequently missed injury' in *American Journal of Radiology* 128, 981.

Dandy, D.J. and Edwards, D.J. (1998). *Essentials of Orthopaedics and Trauma*, 3rd edn. London: Churchill Livingstone.

Greenspan, A. and Gershwin, M.E. (1990). *Radiology of the Arthrides – a Clinical Approach*. London, New York: JB Lippincott, Gower Medical Publishing.

Helms, Clyde A. (1995). *Fundamentals of Skeletal Radiology*, 2nd edn. London: W.B. Saunders.

Keats, T. (2001). *Atlas of Normal Roentgen Variants that may Simulate Disease*, 7th edn. London: Mosby

Landin, L.A. (1983). 'Children's ankle fractures: classification and epidemiology in *Acta Orthopaedica Scandinavica* 54, 634–640.

Manaster, B.J. (1989). *Handbooks in Radiology; Skeletal Radiology.* London:Year Book Medical Publishers.

NICE (2003). Updated September 2007. *Managing Head Injury: NICE Guidelines.* London: National Institute for Health and Clinical Excellence.

Nicholson, D.A. and Driscoll, P.A. (1995) *ABC of Emergency Radiology*. London: W.B. Saunders.

Ozonoff, M.B. (1979). *Paediatric Orthopaediac Radiology*. Philadelphia: W.B. Saunders.

Pang, D. and Wilerger, J.E. (1982). 'Spinal cord injury without radiographic abnormalities in children' in *Journal of Neurosurgery* 57; 114–129.

Raby, N. and de Lacey, G., (2005). *Accident and Emergency Radiology: A Survival Guide*, 2nd edn. London: Elsevier.

Renton, P. (1998). *Orthopaediac Radiology – Pattern Recognition and Differential Diagnosis*, 2nd edn. London: Martin Dunitz.

Resnick, R. (1989). 'Diagnostic imaging of paediatric skeletal trauma' in *Radiologic Clinics of North America* 27(5), 243–9.

Rogers, L.F. (1992). *Radiology of Skeletal Trauma*, 2nd edn. London: Churchill Livingstone.

Royal College of Radiologists (2003). *Making the Best Use of a Department of Clinical Radiology*, 4th edn. London: RCR.

Salter, R.B. and Harris, W.R. (1963). 'Injuries involving the epiphyseal plate' in *Journal of Bone and Joint Surgery*, 45A, 587.

Stoker, D.J. and Tilley, E.A. (1989). *Self Assessment in Radiology and Imaging 4 – Orthopaedics*. London: Wolfe Medical Publications Ltd.

Thornton, A, and Gyll, C. (1999). *Children's Fractures*. London: W.B. Saunders.

Tile, M. (1995). *Fractures of the Pelvis and Acetabulum*. Baltimore: Williams and Wilkins.

Tile, M. and Pennal, G.F. (1980). 'Pelvic disruption: principles of management' in *Clinical Orthopaedics* 151, 56.